Kindled Terraces

KINDLED *terraces*

American Poets in Greece

Edited by DON SCHOFIELD

TRUMAN STATE UNIVERSITY PRESS
NEW ODYSSEY SERIES

© 2004 Truman State University Press
All rights reserved
New Odyssey Series
Published 2004 by Truman State University Press, Kirksville, Missouri 63501
tsup.truman.edu

Cover photography by Don Schofield; Aegina, Temple of Aphaia; Crete.
Cover designed by Teresa Wheeler
Body type: LegacySerITC by URW Software
Printed by Thomson-Shore, Dexter, Michigan USA

Library of Congress Cataloging-in-Publication Data
Kindled terraces : American poets in Greece / edited by Don Schofield
      p. cm. — (New odyssey series)
   Includes index.
   ISBN 1-931112-37-1 (alk. paper)
   1. Greece—Poetry. 2. Americans—Greece—Poetry. 3. American poetry—20th
century. I. Schofield, Don. II. Series.
   PS595.G77K56 2004
   811'.54—dc22
                                                        2004001714

For Edmund Keeley,
whose love of Greece and its literature
opened the door for so many.

Contents

ACKNOWLEDGMENTS

The editor expresses his heartfelt thanks to the poets whose works appear in this anthology and to their publishers. Without their generosity this book could not have been made. Thanks also to the Virginia Center for the Creative Arts, the Ragdale Foundation, and the Hellenic Studies Program of Princeton University for providing time and space in which to work; to Rachel Hadas, Dimitris Gondicas, Alicia Stallings, and Dino Siotis for their helpful suggestions; David Mason and Moira Egan for their prose contributions to the anthology; John Zervos and Glenn Tornell for the photographs they uncovered; and Litsa Papalexia for her help with the proofs. A special thanks as well to Linda Gregg, whose encouragement and wisdom were essential to the completion of this project.

INTRODUCTION

"If I am a poet, the air of Greece has made me one," Lord Byron declared almost two centuries ago. While most of the forty contemporary American poets included in this anthology wouldn't have taken Byron's words literally, each of them in his or her own way has been inspired by Greece, enough to leave the comforts and familiarity of home and to journey to this small, eastern Mediterranean land—and write about the experience for years to come. But why Greece? What is it about this country of ten million people—until recently the poorest member of the European Union, and with a language known by few others beyond its borders—that gives it a special place in the imaginations of American poets?

The history of Greece is certainly one appeal: its embodiment of the classical legacy. Europeans have been traveling to this land since the time of the Renaissance and North Americans since the eighteenth century, in search of the Golden Age of Hellas, as Greece was known in antiquity. In the English-language tradition a whole body of literature developed from the writings of classicists and philhellenes, a number of whom made pilgrimages to pay homage to the place where Western art, history, and drama, as well as its contradictory traditions of the rational and irrational, and of course its poetry were born. As various regions of Greece rose up against the colonial rule of the Ottoman Empire in the early and middle nineteenth century, Lord Byron and other European philhellenes came to fight alongside the Greeks in an effort to liberate the lands identified with Hellas. They dreamed of a revival of the Golden Age. Many American writers also shared that dream. Some, like Susan Ward Howe, author of "The Battle Hymn of the Republic," even campaigned to raise money and journeyed to Greece to bring relief supplies for refugees caught up in the decades-long struggle.

In more peaceful times Herman Melville and Mark Twain visited and wrote about their experiences, as did poets Hilda Doolittle and Trumball Stickney in the early twentieth century—each fascinated by the evocations of antiquity they encountered, so much so that they often didn't see, or in some cases were repulsed by, the actual Greece standing before them. Mark Twain, for example, described in *Innocents Abroad* the landscape of Attica as a "barren, desolate, unpoetical waste" and the local residents as a "community of questionable characters...confiscators and falsifiers of high repute."

By the 1950s, when this anthology commences, this way of framing Greece started expanding to take in other historical epochs. While thousands of American tourists, enamored of the classical legacy, began flooding into Greece each year, those visitors who cared to look closely were drawn to ruins and artifacts that dated as far back as the Neolithic age and were offered glimpses of Cycladic and Minoan civilizations, along with Mycenaean, Hellenic, Hellenistic, Roman, and Byzantine culture. Each age sparked the imaginations of those receptive to it. Moreover, as many poems in this collection attest, each period left its mark, not only on the landscape, but also on the language and culture of the country's modern inhabitants.

Around the same time a different way of seeing Greece came to the fore— Greece as Paradise. Taking their lead from *Colossus of Maroussi*, Henry Miller's account of his travels through Greece in 1939, as well as from the writings of British expatriate Lawrence Durrell, the work of nineteenth-century English painter and author Edward Lear, and (later) English translations and a film version of Nikos Kazantzakis' *Zorba the Greek*, a whole generation of American poets traveled to Greece in the 1950s, 1960s, and 1970s looking for island Greece. They ventured to Ios, Paros, Crete, and elsewhere, eager to find an alternative to what Miller called "the air conditioned nightmare" of America. Greece seemed to offer these visitors—many of whom chose to stay in remote areas, often without electricity or running water—what America lacked: a pristine, vibrant landscape where they could remain free of the distractions and pressures of the modern world. Living in the mesmerizing light of the Aegean, among people whose lives seemed attuned to the natural rhythms of the seasons and the rituals connected to them, these sojourners saw writing not as a career choice, but as a sacred act as timeless and essential as drawing water from a well.

Other contributors to this collection came in search of their Greek roots, to visit the monasteries of Mount Athos, or to be with a spouse. Some were attracted to urban Greece because of the more relaxed attitude toward homosexuality they found or because life in general seemed freer and the people warmer and more self-expressive. As poets many were inspired to visit or even move to Greece by translations of Constantine Cavafy, Yiannis Ritsos, Nobel Prize winners George Seferis and Odysseus Elytis, and other modern Greek poets. They also were drawn by the prose of British philhellenes Patrick Leigh Fermor and Philip Sherrard and the American expatriate Kevin Andrews. By the 1980s and 1990s, more and more who came began to embrace Greece, not only for its past, but also for the diversity of its present, which they found to be an inspiring admixture of the European, Balkan, Mediterranean, and Oriental.

Whatever motivated the poets presented in this anthology to tour, to return time and again, or to settle here for years—as more than half the poets herein have done—they certainly are not the only ones to have made the journey. This volume easily could be much larger and still not include all the American poets who have come to Greece in recent decades. In assembling this anthology, then, certain choices had to be made, sometimes with difficulty. The time frame was relatively easy to define: I wanted to include poets from the 1950s to the present in order to show how rich and vital writing out of the Greek experience has become. Far more difficult was deciding whom to consider an "American" poet. Any line I drew wound up excluding important figures. Ultimately, I decided not to include poets living in America who were born in Greece. This necessitated leaving out Olga Broumas, Nanos Valaoritis, and other Greek-Americans writing in English. I regret their absence. Collectively they would make up a fine anthology all their own, a project someone should take on in the near future. I also chose to include as "American" three poets born outside the United States (one in Vietnam and two in England) because of the distinctly American voice in their poetry and the fact that each has spent a number of years in both the United States and Greece.

Within these parameters I chose poets who represent a gamut of exposure to Greece, from those who toured for a couple weeks or so, to those who have spent years, even decades, in Greece—with an emphasis on the latter. I also tried to be as geographically representative of Greece as possible, including poets who have lived on the islands, in mainland rural areas and towns, and in the two major cities, Athens and Thessaloniki. To provide a degree of historical perspective I ordered the poets according to the decades they first encountered and started writing about Greece.

As for the criteria used in selecting individual work, first and foremost I wanted each choice to stand well as a poem, not simply as a depiction of some aspect of Greece. I also wanted poems that represent a variety of contemporary styles, voices, and aesthetic approaches in order to show the range of poets drawn to this corner of the eastern Mediterranean. Finally, I wanted poems that offer diverse images of Greece in order to suggest its multiplicity, as well as to indicate the different ways we as Americans approach the foreign and what that says about us, our culture, identity, and poetics. For, besides the reading pleasure and glimpses of the exotic it might offer, a collection such as this can't help but suggest that the way we frame the Other tells us as much about the place we leave as it does about the places to which we journey. Equally important is how the body of work assembled here reveals what is brought back, not so much in our physical return as in the language in which we continue to write.

Don Schofield
Drosia, Athens, June 21, 2003

James Merrill

Greek light strikes the alien eye strongly, irrevocably. It's no surprise to find many images of light in Merrill's Greek poems. "Light into the olive entered / And was oil," opens "After Greece," his poem that clearly bespeaks the dislocation, the poignancy of leaving that light-soaked landscape, to surviving "its meanings, and [his] own." The myriad shades of blue, the trembling rain-pools even at night, the "polychrome relief" of the Metro bar: All are expressions of the poet's urge to imbue the poems themselves with that Hellenic light, to describe the "polychrome relief" of the very landscape.

Merrill, master of form and language, was obviously up to the task. That level of formal grace shows, among other things, Merrill's deep sensitivity to languages. A polyglot, Merrill learned Greek too, rather fluently, which is clear in the poems composed after his time in Greece. For the linguistically sensitive, English-language poet, Modern Greek offers an odd experience. Like meeting a third cousin once removed, and finding in him many of the same odd traits that one has inherited from those same grandparents, one hears in Modern Greek the alternative development of the roots that led to English. For the poet immersed newly in this cacophony, "goods, bads, kaló-kakó," the echolalia is indeed sweet and nourishing.

Siren, fishwife, Modern Greek provided a linguistic home for Merrill just as Greece itself gave him comfort, a sense of family, a home. He lavishes great affection on the Greeks, such as Maria and Kostas Tympakianakis, who appear in the poems; even Kyria Kleo, portrayed not so beautifully in her Dionysian mask, is asked to forgive him should she ever know of the poem. This warm acceptance of the Greeks reciprocated what he himself felt from them: His time in Athens gave him the chance to live what felt like a "normal" life, and clearly he used it well, surrounding himself with friends and writing prolifically.

Merrill's prolificacy was helped by the time he spent in Greece. Poets seem constitutionally to be well aware of their own mortality; it is as if those "Graces, Furies, Fates" (who of course knew Latin as well) whisper, "*Carpe diem,* Poet, for when you die, you will produce no more." To live for any amount of time in Greece is to redefine yourself as part of an ongoing, ever-present history. "You'll see a different cosmos through the eyes of a Greek," true, but you see a different cosmos through your own, newly Hellenized eyes. "The old ideas / found lying open to the elements" inspire one to be sure to leave one's own ideas behind. The click, click of the *Komboloi* marks the passing of time, "grimly / Sanguine with siftings from the great / Cracked hourglass."

Grim and sanguine both, Greeks have lived through occupation and war and continue to move through daily life. Merrill saw and celebrated this day to day in his poems. And not unlike James Joyce, who takes us out of his own Odyssey with Molly Bloom's emphatic "yes," Merrill himself left Greece with the unusual Greek Yes, that "sideways flicker, half headshake of doubt— / Meaning, confusingly, assent." Greece gave him love, language, light in abundance. And in repayment, to himself and to the Greeks: "into the grave I'll wear that Yes of theirs."

Moira Egan

After Greece

Light into the olive entered
And was oil. Rain made the huge pale stones
Shine from within. The moon turned his hair white
Who next stepped from between the columns,
Shielding his eyes. All through
The countryside were old ideas
Found lying open to the elements.
Of the gods' houses only
A minor premise here and there
Would be balancing the heaven of fixed stars
Upon a Doric capital. The rest
Lay spilled, their fluted drums half sunk in cyclamen
Or deep in water's biting clarity
Which just barely upheld me
The next week, when I sailed for home.
But where is home—these walls?
These limbs? The very spaniel underfoot
Races in sleep, toward what?
It is autumn. I did not invite
Those guests, windy and brittle, who drink my liquor.

Returning from a walk I find
The bottles filled with spleen, my room itself
Smeared by reflection onto the far hemlocks.
I some days flee in dream
Back to the exposed porch of the maidens
Only to find my great-great-grandmothers
Erect there, peering
Into a globe of red Bohemian glass.
As it swells and sinks, I call up
Graces, Furies, Fates, removed
To my country's warm, lit halls, with rivets forced
Through drapery, and nothing left to bear.
They seem anxious to know
What holds up heaven nowadays.
I start explaining how in that vast fire
Were other irons—well, Art, Public Spirit,
Ignorance, Economics, Love of Self,
Hatred of Self, a hundred more,
Each burning to be felt, each dedicated
Toll sparing us the worst; how I distrust them
As I should have done those ladies; how I want
Essentials: salt, wine, olive, the light, the scream—
No! I have scarcely named you,
And look, in a flash you stand full-grown before me,
Row upon row, Essentials,
Dressed like your sister caryatids
Or tombstone angels, jealous of their dead,
With undulant coiffures, lips weathered, cracked by grime,
And faultless eyes gone blank beneath the immense
Zinc and gunmetal northern sky...
Stay then. Perhaps the system
Calls for spirits. The first glass I down
To the last time
I ate and drank in that old world. May I
Also survive its meanings, and my own.

Days of 1964

Houses, an embassy, the hospital,
Our neighborhood sun-cured if trembling still
In pools of the night's rain...
Across the street that led to the center of town
A steep hill kept one company part way
Or could be climbed in twenty minutes
For some literally breathtaking views,
Framed by umbrella pines, of city and sea.
Underfoot, cyclamen, autumn crocus grew
Spangled as with fine sweat among the relics
Of good times had by all. If not Olympus,
An out-of-earshot, year-round hillside revel.

I brought home flowers from my climbs.
Kyria Kleo who cleans for us
Put them in water, sighing *Virgin, Virgin.*
Her legs hurt. She wore brown, was fat, past fifty,
And looked like a Palmyra matron
Copied in lard and horsehair. How she loved
You, me, loves us all, the bird, the cat!
I think now she *was* love. She sighed and glistened
All day with it, or pain, or both.
(We did not notably communicate.)
She lived nearby with her pious mother
And wastrel son. She called me her real son.

I paid her generously, I dare say.
Love makes one generous. Look at us. We'd known
Each other so briefly that instead of sleeping
We lay whole nights, open, in the lamplight,
And gazed, or traded stories.

One hour comes back—you gasping in my arms
With love, or laughter, or both,
I having just remembered and told you
What I'd looked up to see on my way downtown at noon:
Poor old Kleo, her aching legs,
Trudging into the pines. I called,
Called three times before she turned.
Above the tight, skyblue sweater, her face

Was painted. Yes. Her face was painted
Clown-white, white of the moon by daylight,
Lidded with pearl, mouth a poinsettia leaf,
Eat me, pay me—the erotic mask
Worn the world over by illusion
To weddings of itself and simple need.

Startled mute, we had stared—was love illusion?—
And gone our ways. Next, I was crossing a square
In which a moveable outdoor market's
Vegetables, chickens, pottery kept materializing
Through a dream-press of hagglers each at heart
Leery lest he be taken, plucked,
The bird, the flower of that November mildness,
Self lost up soft clay paths, or found, foothold,
Where the bud throbs awake
The better to be nipped, self on its knees in mud—
Here I stopped cold, for both our sakes;

And calmer on my way home bought us fruit.

Forgive me if you read this. (And may Kleo,
Should someone ever put it into Greek
And read it aloud to her, forgive me, too.)
I had gone so long without loving,
I hardly knew what I was thinking.

Where I hid my face, your touch, quick, merciful,
Blindfolded me. A god breathed from my lips.
If that was illusion, I wanted it to last long;
To dwell, for its daily pittance, with us there,
Cleaning and watering, sighing with love or pain.
I hoped it would climb when it needed to the heights
Even of degradation, as I for one
Seemed, those days, to be always climbing
Into a world of wild
Flowers, feasting, tears—or was I falling, legs
Buckling, heights, depths,
Into a pool of each night's rain?
But you were everywhere beside me, masked,
As who was not, in laughter, pain and love.

The "Metro"

One level below street, an airless tank—
We'd go there, evening, watch through glass the world
Eddy by, winking, casting up
Such gorgeous flotsam that hearts leapt, or sank.

Over the bar, in polychrome relief,
A jungle idyll: tiger, water hole,
Mate lolling on her branch apéritif-
Green eyes aglare. We also lolled and drank,

Joking with scarface Kosta, destitute
Sotíri, Plato in his new striped suit...
Those tigers are no more now. The bar's gone,
And in its place, O memory! a bank

More Enterprise

A sideways flicker, half headshake of doubt—
Meaning, confusingly, assent—fills out
The scant wardrobe of gesture I still use.
It clings by habit now. The old strait swank
I came in struts the town on local heirs.
Koula's nephew has the suit she shrank,
Andreas coveted my Roman shoes...
Into the grave I'll wear that Yes of theirs.

Komboloi

the Greek "worry-beads"

Begin. Carnation underfoot, tea splashing stars
Onto this mottled slab, amber coherences,

Unmatched string of habitué
Told and retold, rubbed lucid, quick with scenes...

That face—fire-slitted fur, whip fury, slate iced over!
Click. An early life. The warrior's

Came late, enchanted brief. Then, gem on brow
And far-eyed peregrine on wrist,

One life in profile brushed so fine
You felt no single stroke until the last of thousands.

All that while, the bed had flowed, divided,
Deepened and sung in sparkling attacks

None but whose woman brought her warm specific,
Her tongue unspeakable. Click. Taxis

Yoked together floors below were making
Summer hell. Yet from her pupil streamed

Radii such as gall the ferry's shadow
Plunging like my pen past shoals of shilly-shally

Into fathomless gentian. Or into
Some thinnest "shade" of blue

Juniper berries fallen on this far bank
Of now no river. Wingbeats echo where its ghost

Forks. Focus the half mile down
Upon snapped golds—if not a corn plantation

Then a small ill-strung harp which dead hands pluck
And pluck. No sound. No issue. The wheel

Founders in red rainwater, soul inchdeep in pain,
Charred spokesman of reflections grimly

Sanguine with siftings from the great
Cracked hourglass. Click. Will...? Click.

Will second wind come even to the runners
Out of time? These beads—O marble counter—Done.

Kostas Tympakianákis

Sir, friend. We'll be drinking and I'll tell you why.
Today I went to Customs to identify
My brother—it was him, all right, in spite of both
Feet missing from beneath his Army overcoat.

He was a handsome devil twice the size of me.
We're all good-looking in my family.
If you saw that brother, or what's left of him,
You'd understand at once the kind of man he'd been.

I have other brothers, one whose face I broke
In a family quarrel, and that's no joke:
I'm small but strong, when I get mad I fight.
Seven hundred vines of his were mine by right

And still are—fine! He's welcome to them.
I'm twenty-two. It's someone else's turn to dream.
I liked our school and teacher till they made me stop
And earn my living in a welder's shop.

Cousins and friends were learning jokes and games
At the Kafeneíon behind steamed-up panes.
I worked without a mask in a cold rain of sparks
That fell on you and burned—look, you can still see marks.

The German officer stubbed his *puro* out
On my mother's nipples but her mouth stayed shut.
She lived to bear me with one foot in the grave
And they never found my father in his mountain cave.

He died last year at eighty. To his funeral
Came a NATO Captain and an English General.
Our name is known around Herakleion
In all the hill towns, just ask anyone.

Outside our village up above Knossós
A railed-in plot of cypresses belongs to us,
Where we'll put my brother and if there's room
One day I'll lie beside him till the crack of doom.

But I'd rather travel to a far-off land,
Though I never shall, and settle, do you understand?
The trouble here is not with sun and soil
So much as meanness in the human soul.

I worked a time in Germany, I saw a whore
Smile at me from inside her little lighted door.
She didn't want my money, she was kind and clean
With mirrors we submerged in like a submarine.

The girl I loved left me for a Rhodiot.
I should be broken-hearted, but it's strange, I'm not.
Take me with you when you sail next week,
You'll see a different cosmos through the eyes of a Greek.

Or write my story down for people. Use my name.
And may it bring you all the wealth and fame
It hasn't brought its bearer. Here, let's drink our wine!
Who could have imagined such a life as mine?

To My Greek

Dear nut
Uncrackable by nuance or debate,
Eat with your fingers, wear your bloomers to bed,

Under my skin stay nude. Let past and future

Perish upon our lips, ocean inherit
Those paper millions. Let there be no word
For justice, grief, convention; *you* be convention—
Goods, bads, kaló-kakó, cockatoo-racous

Coastline of white printless coves

Already strewn with offbeat echolalia.
Forbidden Salt Kiss Wardrobe Foot Cloud Peach
—Name it, my chin drips sugar. Radiant dumbbell, each

Noon's menus and small talk leave you

Likelier, each sunset yawned away,
Hair in eyes, head bent above the strummed
Lexicon, gets by heart about to fail
This or that novel mode of being together

Without conjunctions. Still

I fear for us. Nights fall
We toss through blindly, drenched in her appraising
Glare, the sibyl I turn to

When all else fails me, when you do—

The mother tongue!
Her least slip a mirror triptych of glosses,
Her automation and my mind are one.
Ancient in fishscale silver-blue,

What can she make of you? Her cocktail sweats

With reason: speech will rise from it,
Quite beyond your comprehension rise
Like blood to a slapped face, stingingly apt

If unrepeatable, tones one forgets

Even as one is changed for life by them,
Veins branching a cold coral,
Common sense veering into common scenes,
Tears, incoherent artifice,

Altar upset, cut glass and opaline

Schools ricocheting through the loud cave
Where lie my Latin's rusted treasure,
The bones, picked clean, of my Italian,

Where some blue morning also she may damn

Well find her windpipe slit with that same rainbow
Edge a mere weekend with you gives

To books, to living (anything to forego
That final drunken prophecy whereby,

Lacking her blessing, you my siren grow

Stout, serviceable, gray.
A fishwife shawled in fourth-hand idiom
Spouting my views to earth and heaven)—Oh,

Having chosen the way of little knowledge,

Trusted each to use the other
Kindly except in moments of gross need,
Come put the verb-wheel down
And kiss my mouth despite the foot in it.

Let schoolboys brave her shallows. Sheer

Lilting azure float them well above
Those depths the surfacer
Lives, when he does, alone to sound and sound.

The barest word be what I say in you.

ALAN ANSEN

More than influencing Alan Ansen's poetry, Greece has provided a refuge for this "Classical scholar in Beat's clothing, [this] joy popper with

John Zervos

monastic discipline," as Stephen Moore describes him in his Introduction to *Contact Highs: Selected Poems 1957–1987.* Ansen started coming to Greece in the 1950s, making frequent visits while living in Venice, and later regularly spending winters in warmer, dryer Athens. He moved to Greece permanently in 1961 after being expelled from Venice in a police crackdown on homosexuality.

Once in Athens Ansen took up residence, as Rachel Hadas recalls in her Afterword to *Contact Highs,* in a "[t]all old house (since demolished) on Alopekis Street in Kolonaki, walls covered with Corso collages, looming bookshelves and drooping gladioli, lilies, freesias bought weekly from the Friday market and watered daily." He chose Athens because, in contrast to Venice, "people here don't worry about *bella figura* ...and they take personal relationships more seriously." Those relationships include lifelong associations with members of two opposing literary camps, "pale faces" and "red skins," as Ansen is fond of characterizing them. Among the former, James Merrill and Chester Kallman, W.H. Auden's companion of many years, took up residence in Athens in the 1960s and 1970s for extended periods of time. From the latter, Gregory Corso, William S. Burroughs, Allen Ginsberg, and other friends from the Beat Movement paid intermittent visits. Ansen's love of classical literature and the poetry of Constantine Cavafy also made Greece appealing, as did the opportunity to have his masques, often dedicated to various friends, performed.

The contrasts that characterize Ansen's friendships over the years also can be seen in his poetry. "By instinct and biographical compulsion, I want the naked scream," he says in reflecting on *Disorderly Houses,* his first book published in America, "By training and remembered satisfactions, I

12

utter patterns." Rachel Hadas describes his poetry as a "raucous yawp ... [that] is regularly redeemed from barbarity (however much Ansen yearns to be brutish) by its reverence for its own medium—for many of Ansen's poems are majestically solipsistic broodings on their own occasions. To meditate on life and art, on influence and poetics, at the top of one's lungs, with supreme intelligence and self-consciousness—well, the paradoxes don't stop."

Due to ill health Ansen rarely leaves home these days. His closest friends among the Beats have passed away, as have his companions from the opposite camp. Nevertheless, other friends surround the man who appears as Rollo Grebin in Jack Kerouac's *On the Road* and as A.J. in Burroughs' *Naked Lunch*. Visiting poets and scholars seek out the legendary figure to whom Auden dedicated his 1950 book, *The Enchafed Flood,* and who was Auden's lover's most devoted friend after the poet died, and so describes himself in "Epistle to Chester Kallman" as the "keeper of the keeper of the Flame." A distinguished elder among American expatriates, Alan Ansen is visited and cared for these days by a whole new generation of "red skins" and "pale faces."

Don Schofield

Moving

For Kosta, Vassili, Babis and Angelos

1

An old man's comforts, twelve long years of tenancy,
A place for everything and everything
In its place, a growing sense of a lieutenancy
Untouchable, deferential, catering
To easy flow, arthritic crotchets, jets
And callid composition of sestets.

Sand in the KY, gradual disparition
Of warmer younger bodies once familiar,
Trolling the darker shades of inanition,
Renders complacence semiatrabiliar
Driving it forth to saunters in the night
A wheezing hobbling would-be catamite

Intermittently successful in his quest
For inexpensive sex, a compromise
Of his ideal at the cool behest

Of available reality to revise
His senses' syndromes, grudgingly accept
What age allows him dogged if inept.

2

When suddenly the summons to vacate the premises galvanizes the ganglia as it paralyzes the spirit.
The numb pursuit of vocation under the dead weight of Damocles.
Then the walk, scurry and trudge around the neighborhood and the scanning of the classifieds in search of something
Found suddenly—a lesser green and a real balcony instead of the overwhelming cascade of pines, a real janitor for the amateur block warden, a long corridor plus more but smaller rooms
And movers from the middle distance; but he puts off the evil hour.

Meanwhile, sick, sorry and distraught, he stumps the park as in the far-off days when the draft impended—*vogue la galère!*
At first, a suave substantial expensive presence.
Then a teen trio, green in the green, met, welcomed and swallowed in the wilder shades of a desperate shift
Renewing the pains and pleasures of youth at a loose end,
Diverting the pains of transition with compensatory strain:
Fresh skin for the snake as it sheds its old one,
Bright eyes for the myopic groper in the vague.

Meanwhile the motions of moving: metal bookcases measured, selected and installed.
Then the books: unshelved, transported and installed.
Finally the furniture and fine art: freighted, positioned and hung with a minimum of fuss (but some fuss there was) and at considerable expense.

3

And now the numbness and disorientation
Dimly registering the losses in slow motion,
Cheered by the boys, by booze and by detective stories,
By solitaire practiced with a zombie's zealousness,
One gropes one's way from back to front, back again to bed,
The heavy haven of the lacerated spirit.
Gradually in the course of months as revival,
Niggling but perceptible, permits the resumption

Of old routines and the tentative acquisition
Of new shopping habits and even a few more books,
Poetry itself seems once more possible, the air
Is still the air of Lycabbetus, the balcony
Is a new if intermittent grace with a view of trees,
Of flowers, of Hymettus to be shared with the cats,
My most important, my most intimate new neighbors,
To be tolerated, cleaned up after but not fed.
The human neighbors too seem mild and inoffensive,
But the losses remain—a library of lacunas,
A sense of spaces growing cozy but not sacred,
The rescission of flowers and the weekly market,
A fitting place for the great C minus of this life.

Cats

As the boys fade out the cats fade in
Jumping down from the tree, creeping under the partition, delicately walking the
    balcony railing,
Waiting for food, licking themselves, sleeping, spying, enjoying their state,
Modeling the being of God's creatures for a less satisfied one.

No rough and ready dog may invade the balcony's felinity,
Though an obnoxious bark may alert it.

Here one learns courtesy, patience, self-abnegation
Resigning a favorite chair to a cat in possession
Rather than attempting to justify the logic of proprietorship to a sentience
    determined not to understand.
But one is tempted to wrath when a mother pushes her way in to the interior to
    stash her newly born kittens
I didn't make you screech for those kittens;
Let their father, that no-good loafer, go out and rent an apartment for them!

What's the use? Expel the cats with a broomstick they return
Hungry, weary, forgiving, distracting,
An opportunity for love.

Peter Green

Variously a novelist, academic ancient historian, and translator, as well as a poet, I count as my chief influences Aristophanes, Herodotos, Byron, Cavafy, Ritsos, Eliot, and MacNeice, together with the people, landscape, and moods—winter and summer alike—of the eastern Aegean.

Delphi

Here the brightness begins: the sunlight
Streams in over the rocks, the eagle
Poises and planes, remote
From navel-stone or conducted tour,

Bay-leaves and mantic runes. Our insight
Takes an edge from the cleft. Regal,
Divine—the loaded epithets denote
Something archaic and numinous, suddenly pour

The ice of unwilling acceptance through your spine,
Riddle this random moment to a bedrock of foreseeing,
Cash and glory, ephemeral bright lustre
Lighting the body's transcension. Quiet, quiet now,

Apollo's voice a descant of Byzantine sheep-bells, divine
Epiphanies brushed aside by guides and scholars, being
Out of place in museum catalogues, a drag on the bluster
Of some sing-song dogmatist telling you When and How

But seldom Why. Which is why, perhaps, each visit
Has been—for you as for me—a frightening step
Into some too-bright void. Appearances dazzle,
Snow sugars the gorges, ice stabs like fire,

And who, today, holds the knowledge that could elicit
Plain truth from conundrum? Facts, or seeming facts, are cheap.
So let ice burn and melt, your private puzzle
Will find these oracles dumb. Love, go up higher—

The road curves, sunlight spills below on a scattered
Cubage of grey weather stone. The charioteer
Stands at gaze with empty hands, his bronze-hollow eyes lost
In a horseless world where breeding and high endeavor

Are as dead—and obscure—as Pindar, the dogmas shattered,
Dust on the sapless laurel. Slow down, change gear,
Drive up the ramp and park. If there was, maybe, a ghost
Somewhere below, it is gone. But hotels are real, and for ever.

Ikaria

I.

The myth was wrong to begin with—Daedalus had
     No business on this sharpbacked ridge of schist,
The long stone cutthroat razor; wasn't mad,
     Knew Attica from Ionia, northwest from east.

Nature always fought man here, usually won,
     Made him sweat for each toe-hold. The breed came tough
And needed to. Seared by a killing sun,
     Blown endways by the *meltemi,* they had it rough,

Prided themselves on living close to the earth,
     Spurned beds, were reputed savages in furs
By cultured Samians, came to thrive on dearth,
     Sneered at their soft-lying neighbors, jovial sirs

Who spread the joke that when God made these parts
     Ikaria became his trash-heap. But such orts and merds

The islanders put to good use, their obstinate hearts
    Determined to work the unworkable, free as birds

If (despite their name) wingless. Each terrace hacked ·
    From the reluctant hillside, stone by blind stone,
Watched by sardonic goats, became an act
    Of defiance against whatever god had thrown

A scatter of seed on harsh ground: the will to survive
    Facing, and beating, tough odds. But they had to fight
Each step of the way: even to stay alive
    Became a Heraklean labor, an out-of-sight

Wrestling with daemons and outcrops. To advance a mile
    Meant ten slogged to and fro in each valley's v
Under those towering screes, a crunch of red shale,
    Sweat layering dust on the skin, an indifferent bee

Loud in each dab of gold broom, its prickled scent
    A luxury none could afford. Water lay deep
Under the limestone, fed taproots, mocked time spent
    By man the rootless digger. Life came cheap

In a market that barely existed. Want bred pride,
    Conjured a past of blue blood, refused to marry
Outside the island. Byzantine purple dyed
    Their clenched self-reliance, let their bent backs carry

That stone weight of isolation. Like their lean goats
    They ate, built, dreamed, wed what came to hand
In a scrannel world, caught fish from cockle boats,
    Bred square-hipped daughters, bleached skins on harsh sand.

II.

Time-warps are vulnerable. My plane touched down
    On a white slash of runway quarried out
By giant mechanical robots through a frown
    Of rough and crippling rock, a pinched redoubt

Of modern self-assertion. Windgusts whined
    In the airport roof. Outside, a solid wall

Of rough and redcut scarp, neatly aligned
    With sliding glass doors, intimidatingly tall,

Served too well to remind us all that we
    Were here on sufferance. The windsock strained,
Gusts whipped us, canvas thundered. *The will is free?*
    Not on this island. It was necessity reigned

From the beginning, over a handful of dour
    Determined scrabblers. And today reigns still,
With ruined grey stone crofts to show where hope went sour,
    Their crumbling terraces smeared into the hill

And bloodflecked with wild poppies. Rage. Thirst. Death.
    Today? Asphalt smooths our passage, gas replaces
The muscles of man or donkey: not one breath
    That strains the lungs; the car's put through its paces

By steep and angled hairpins, banked blind turns,
    But the driver masters such challenges in the shade,
Not breaking a sweat. Outside, the sun's lens burns
    Leafage and rock, short shadows enfilade

A tinkle of goats on the cliffside. Here urban man
    Makes his moon landing, cocooned in a high-tech bubble,
Immune yet exposed, pursuing some alien plan,
    But still walking warily, bent on avoiding trouble

Piled up by the centuries. When nature briefly slept
    While pots simmered on the hearth, the spiralling smoke
Signalled to pirates, who climbed, stole, burned and raped
    What had survived the winds—a Herrenvolk

In Homer's epic book. His heroic age
    Meant ripping off other men's goods when producing your own
Was too much sweat or trouble. Victims' rage
    Never made it into the *Iliad*. What cuts stone?

III.

What you see is what you get here. Credit cards have no place,
    Hard cash is the sole reality, even if not so hard

As most would prefer. The turbaned and watermarked face
    Of Kolokotronis offers a paper-thin safeguard

Of five thousand drachmas. Ten is out of sight.
    But coins are solid, a comprehensible scale
Stopping short at one hundred, with Alexander to fight
    Their battles for them, the assertive ethnic male

Icon par excellence, lacking only the seal
    Of Orthodox Christendom to win every priest's acclaim,
Recapture the lost City, vanquish the infidel,
    Run the Great Idea up the flagpole, reconsecrate the flame

In Aghia Sophia. Such practical fancies
    Take good root on an island where pirates had their way
Till an eon's breath ago, where our modern advances
    Are on hostile soil, where creative time is away

And somewhere different. One question nags at me: why
    Had this island bred no writers? Muteness or pique,
What was its message? That the self-serving lie
    Is beyond an Ikarian's means? That any oblique

Recreation of harsh reality rests on a dream,
    A margin that never existed? Can no change
Impact this crabbed resistance? Is the seam
    Unworkable to eternity? Must its strange

And stubborn substance present an alien face
    To the world's web for ever? Echo returns
Its dusty answer, a recalcitrant case
    Which—like the sun here—heals less than it burns.

IV.

Looking back on my time here, what do I see?
    Tall windmills stir-mixing the galeblast, clutches of white
Houses crimped into sheer rockfall, slithering scree
    Rolled down by spring floods: the harsh and leaching light

That gives no quarter; the sea a huge untamed cat
    Inviting caresses, yet ready upon a whim

To strike, overwhelm, destroy: a dancing flat
    Surface apt for explosion, a purring rim

Of sundown and sudden storm. But ultimate power
    Remains invisible, a daemon of raging air
That, like faith, can move mountains, uproot forests, scour
    Earth of its comforting maquis, leaving the rock bare;

Can overleap harbor bars, whipping waters to flood,
    Smash eggshell hulls: where Poseidon—or Atlas—laughed
Blaze its random trail of wreckage and mud,
    Archaic godhead incarnate. Odysseus' raft

Knew Poiseidon's anger: the names may have changed
    But the fury endures, is timeless. And timelessness
Is here of the essence, an eternal struggle ranged
    Against historical clutter, the thrust and press

Of movement, conquest, growth. Happy the land
    (They say) without history. But there are worse
Devils here than mankind, an angry ampersand
    From the Big Bang to these rocks, a primal curse

Compounded and elemental, as indifferent to
    The breath of life as a meteor. The *meltemi* scours
Heart and head here, cracks granite. Yet stubbornly through
    The ages one voice persists: *This land is ours.*

Linda Gregg

There will be the smell of Greek sunlight with her when she walks from the train to the tram that goes to Monastiraki Square. She will walk to

the brothel-turned-hotel from there. The next day there will be the smell of crude oil on the freighter from Piraeus to an island. She will be watching almond trees on the mountain for most of the next seven years after that. A goat bleating near its mother by the stone house. The well-cover bangs shut in October. The sea is too strong all winter, roaring even when it's silent. Covering her head completely when she walks to town along the edge of the shore. The shepherd-boy sitting on a table at the back of the taverna, surrounded by happy farmers giving him wine to drink. Buying fresh donuts from the man carrying them through the village on his head every Monday. Swimming in the sea all afternoon, then eating the melon. Eight-year-old Stephanie in only the bottom of her bathing suit, standing with great bunches of grapes, laughing and jumping up and down in the aqua water. Walking alone to the mountain where gods have been honored, the brightness of the sun stunning. Seeing broken libation cups in the weeds. Living and alone with the magnitude. So close to the laws of nature.

Hal Lum

The Island of Kos

Nothing but wilderness around.
Two days of spring and then days of cold.
The sea flooding the road.
Wild heaving against poetry.
Breaking boats on the rocks.
Spill, spill and pour against the mountain.
Flooding the winter wheat.

Wait for me! Wait for me! You are far ahead.
I think the wilderness has won. We are silent
in the house while the wind rises and wanes.
I came here not knowing there was something
that could be lost. That could be taken.

In order to get to sleep, I think:
Go to sleep little goat. Your first week is over.
Go to sleep now.

The Poet Goes about Her Business

for Michele (1966–1972)

Michele has become another dead little girl. An easy poem.
Instant Praxitelean. Instant seventy-five year old photograph
of my grandmother when she was a young woman with shadows
I imagine were blue around her eyes. The beauty of it.
Such guarded sweetness. What a greed of bruised gardenias.
Oh Christ, whose name rips silk, I have seen raw cypresses
so dark the mind comes to them without color.
Dark on the Greek hillside. Dark, volcanic, dry and stone.
Where the oldest women of the world are standing dressed in black
up in the branches of fig trees in the gorge
knocking with as much quickness as their weakness will allow.
Weakness which my heart must not confuse with tenderness.
And on the other side of the island a woman
walks up the path with a burden of leaves on her head,
guiding the goats with sounds she makes up,
and then makes up again. The other darkness is easy:
the men in the dreams who come in together to me with knives.
There are so many traps, and many look courageous.
The body goes into such raptures of obedience.
But the huge stones on the desert resemble
nobody's mother. I remember the snake.
After its skin had been cut away, and it was dropped
it started to move across the clearing.
Making its beautiful waving motion.
It was all meat and bone. Pretty soon it was covered with dust.
It seemed to know exactly where it wanted to go.
Toward any dark trees.

Gnostics on Trial

Let us make the test. Say God wants you
to be unhappy. That there is no good.
That there are horrors in store for us
if we do manage to move toward Him.
Say you keep Art in its place, not too high.
And that everything, even eternity, is measurable.
Look at the photographs of the dead,
both natural (one by one) and unnatural
in masses. All tangled. You know about that.
And can put Beauty in its place. Not too high,
and passing. Make love our search for unhappiness,
which is His plan to help us.
Disregard that afternoon breeze from the Aegean
on a body almost asleep in the shuttered room.
Ignore melons, and talking with friends.
Try to keep from rejoicing. Try
to keep from happiness. Just try.

Balancing Everything

When I lie in bed thinking of those years, I often
remember the ships. On the Aegean especially.
Especially at night among the islands or going
to Athens. The beauty of the moon and stillness.
How hard those journeys sometimes were.
The powerful smell of vomit and urine, sweetened
coffee and crude oil when the ship struggled
against the wind. I think of the night
we were going to die in the storm trying to reach
the passenger liner. Huge waves smashing
over our little boat. Jack screaming at the captain
because he hit me in his fear. Old Greek women
hiding their heads in my lap. Like a miracle.
I talked to them with the few words I knew.
Simple things. How it would be all right.
Telling them to look at the lights of their village
at the top of the great cliffs of Santorini,
up in the dark among the stars.

Me and Aphrodite and the Other

She doesn't move and she is stronger than I am.
She makes sounds like winter. When I plead
that I can't hear, she doesn't hear
because of the power coming out of her.
She isn't pretty. Her strength is by will.
Her mind is kept small.

Maybe those months on the mountain were too much.
Aphrodite loved me and I loved her back.
Taking her pomegranates each time I climbed
that starkness. I would search all day
in the heat and would sit finally happy
in the shade of the fig tree with what
I had found of her scant, broken treasures,
the goat bells clattering around as I looked
down through her light to the Aegean. In a daze
of weariness, reverence and clarity.

Now this older one has come. More ancient,
tougher, less complete and fine as can be.
She has come thinking I am strong enough,
though I sit on the curbs crying
without knowledge, without control.
Sees my mouth open and my agony.
If she can, she will destroy my life.
If she can't, I'll try again to be married.

The Design Inside Them

At six every night the women sit on chairs
under vine leaves or out on the street in front
of the houses on whitewashed rocks crocheting.
The talk in Greek is too fast for me, but I can tell
it is about prices in Mytilene compared to here.
They make pictures of flowers and leaves and birds
with white string to cover the windows,
tables and pillows. One of the women serves me
a piece of cake in syrup and a glass of water.

A daughter comes through the billowing curtain
in the doorway. She is fifteen and wants a Walkman
and goes away. She will never be like them.
Her little sister goes from the mother and stands
near a man who is feeding olive branches to his goat.
Then to the new kittens and back to her mother.
Sits quiet in the chatter and industry, and then away
again to the kittens and the man. As though
a string is tied to her waist and unravels like
their idea of justice and good and gentle kindness.
Gathers up again as the old swallows and flowers.

Hephaestus Alone

His heart is like a boat that sets forth alone
on the ocean and goes far out from him,
as Aphrodite proceeds on her pleasure journeys.
He pours the gold down the runnels
into a great mystery under the sand.
When he pulls it up by the feet
and knocks off the scale, it is a god.
What is it she finds with those men
that equals this dark birthing? He makes
each immortal manifest. The deities
remain invisible in their pretty gardens
of grass and violets, of daffodils and jasmine.
Even his wife lives like that. Going on yachts,
speaking to the captains in the familiar.
Let them have it, the noons and rain and joy.
He makes a world here out of frog songs
and packed earth. He made his wife
so she contains the green-fleshed
melons of Lindos, thalo blue of the sea,
and one ripe peach at five in the morning.
He fashioned her by the rules, with love,
made her with rage and disillusion.

Not a Pretty Bird

She was not a nightingale
as the Greek said.
Philomela was a woman.
The sister of the new wife.
Raped, tongue cut out by the husband.
Locked away.
Not a swallow, not the bird of morning
and late evenings that end so swiftly.
Not a myth. She was a girl.
That is the story: the empty mouth,
the bloody breasts. The outrage.
Not the transformation.

Jack Gilbert

The profit for me in the years I lived on the Greek islands was the look of things. Greece was very poor back then. It felt stripped. Only  essentials. The rocks were stone, the Aegean was water, the Greek sun came up and the sun went down. The big stars were far away. Farming was painfully unrewarding. Scant soil and almost no water. Never laughter in the fields. (The Greeks went to town to laugh.) There were never women lying on the beaches. And no sound of cars, because there were so few cars. A world of beautiful bareness. Only the purity and a sense of the gods being alive in the earth. The smell of the gods being alive in the earth. The smell of oregano and sage. "When not adorned adorned the most." Living in the village, and then the fields and finally the mountains as a kind of arriving. The abundance of very little. Where even the loneliness was fine.

Finding Eurydice

Orpheus is too old for it now. His famous voice is gone
and his career is past. No profit anymore from the songs
of love and grief. Nobody listens. Still, he goes on
secretly with his ruined alto. But not for Eurydice.
Not even for the pleasure of singing. He sings because
that is what he does. He sings about two elderly
Portuguese men in the hot Sacramento delta country.
How they show up every year or so, feeble and dressed
as well as their poverty allows. The husband is annoyed
each time by their coming to see his seventy-year-old
wife, who, long ago when they were putting through

the first railroads, was the most beautiful of all
the whores. Impatient, but saying nothing, he lets them
take her carefully upstairs to give her a bath. He does
not understand how much their doting eyes can see the sleek,
gleaming beauty of her hidden in the bright water.

The Edge of the World

I light the lamp and look at my watch.
Four-thirty. Tap out my shoes
because of the scorpions, and go out
into the field. Such a sweet night.
No moon, but urgent stars. Go back inside
and make hot chocolate on my butane burner.
I search around with the radio through
the skirl of the Levant. "Tea for Two"
in German. Finally, Cleveland playing
the Rams in the rain. It makes me feel
acutely here and everybody somewhere else.

All the Way from There to Here

From my hill I look down on the freeway and over
to a gull lifting black against the grey ridge.
It lifts slowly higher and enters the bright sky.
Surely our long, steady dying brings us to a state
of grace. What else can I call this bafflement?

From here I deal with my irrelevance to love.
With the bewildering tenderness of which I am
composed. The sun goes down and comes up again.
The moon comes up and goes down. I live
with the morning air and the different airs of night.
I begin to grow old.

The ships put out and are lost.
Put out and are lost.
Leaving me with their haunting awkwardness
and the imperfection of birds. While all the time
I work to understand this happiness I have come into.

What I remember of my nine-story fall
down the great fir is the rush of green.
And the softness of my regret in the ambulance going
to my nearby death, looking out at the trees leaving me.

What I remember of my crushed spine
is seeing Linda again and again,
sliding down the white X-ray room wall
as my sweet body flailed on the steel table
unable to manage the bulk of pain. That
and waiting in the years after for the burning
in my fingertips, which would announce,
the doctors said, the beginning of paralysis.

What I remember best of the four years of watching
in Greece and Denmark and London and Greece is Linda
making lunch. Her blondeness and ivory coming up
out of the blue Aegean, Linda walking with me daily
across the island from Monolithos to Thíra and back.
That's what I remember most of death:
the gentleness of us in that bare Greek Eden,
the beauty as the marriage steadily failed.

The History of Men

It thrashes in the oaks and soughs in the elms,
Catches on innocence and soon dismantles that.
Sends children bewildered into life. Childhood
ends and is not buried. The young men ride out
and fall off, the horses wandering away. They get
on boats, are carried downstream, discover maidens.
They marry them without meaning to, meaning no harm,
the language beyond them. So everything ends.
Divorce gets them nowhere. They drift away from
the ruined women without noticing. See birds
high up and follow. "Out of earshot," they think,
puzzled by *earshot*. History driving them forward,
making a noise like the wind in maples, of women
in their dresses. It stings their hearts finally.
It wakes them up, baffled in the middle of their lives

on a small bare island, the sea blue and empty,
the days stretching all the way to the horizon.

Ghosts

I heard a noise this morning and found two old men
leaning on the wall of my vineyard, looking out
over the fields, silent. Went back to my desk
until somebody raised the trap door of the well.
It was the one with the cane, looking down inside.
But I was annoyed when the locked door rattled where
the grain and wine were. Went to the kitchen window
and stared at him. He said something in Greek.
I spread my arms to ask what he was doing.
He explained about growing up out there long ago.
That now they were making a little walk among
the old places. Telling it with his hands.
He made a final gesture, rubbing the side
of the first finger against that of the other.
I think it meant how much he felt about being here
again. We smiled, even though he was half blind.
Later, my bucket banged and I saw the heavy one
pulling up water. He cleaned the mule's stone basin
carefully with his other hand. Put back a rock
for the doves to stand on and poured in fresh water.
Stayed there, touching the old letters cut in the marble.
I watched them go slowly down the land and out
of sight. They did not look back. As I typed,
I listened for the dog at each farm to tell me
which house they went to next. But the dogs did not
bark all the way down the long bright alley.

On Stone

The monks petition to live the harder way,
in pits farther up the mountain,
but only the favored ones are permitted
that scraped life. The syrup-water and cakes
the abbot served me were far too sweet.
A simple misunderstanding of pleasure

because of inexperience. I pull water up
hand over hand from thirty feet of stone.
My kerosene lamp burns a mineral light.
The mind and its fierceness lives here in silence.
I dream of women and hunger in my valley
for what can be made of granite. Like the sun
hammering this earth into pomegranates
and grapes. Dryness giving way to the smell
of basil at night. Otherwise, the stone
feeds on stone, is reborn as rock,
and the heart wanes. Athena's owl calling
into the barrenness, and nothing answering.

EDWARD FIELD

When I arrived in Greece in 1949, I instantly felt more at home than anywhere I'd ever been. It was as though I had found my people. Equally important, I was introduced by friends to the poetry of Constantine Cavafy, which changed my own poetry forever. Cavafy's poetry seemed to me an organic part of the deeply human culture around me with its roots in the classical world. His tone only could have grown out of the Greek life I was experiencing, where people talked to each other, treated each other with an intimacy that embraced each other, and where, astonishing to me as a homosexual, men were not afraid of each other, as in the United States where the fear of homosexuality keeps men apart—antagonistic and competitive, suspicious of their tender feelings.

Louis Field

I was rapidly learning to speak Greek, memorizing my phrase book and talking to everyone in sight. The civil war was still on, and wherever I traveled I was questioned at length by the police, who disbelieved my U.S. passport because I spoke Greek—they thought my accent was that of "a far island." This gave me good practice, and I soon was able to puzzle out Cavafy's poems for myself. Cavafy's language, combining Classical Greek with the Modern and Demotic, gave me a clue how to incorporate into my own poetry my Jewish background with its ancient traditions and *shtetl* informality, the Yiddish inflections of my parents' English, and the popular speech forms of American everyday life. And far from being ashamed of his sexual feelings, as I had been, Cavafy's romantic love poems honored the homosexual impulse as noble, which was completely at variance with the then-homophobic rule in English/American literature. There was also a use of narrative that deeply affected me, one I felt had been abandoned by modern poetry in the West.

For six months I was immersed in Greek life, and when I ran out of money I was fed every day by the great actress Marika Kotopouli, earned enough for my hotel bill by posing for artists, and though raggedly dressed, was treated with respect because I was a poet. My poetry took a great leap forward, and it is with those poems written out of my time in Greece that I opened my first book, *Stand Up, Friend, with Me*, published in 1963.

Donkeys

They are not silent like workhorses
Who are happy or indifferent about the plow and wagon;
Donkeys don't submit like that
For they are sensitive
And cry continually under their burdens;
Yes, they are animals of sensibility
Even if they aren't intelligent enough
To count money or discuss religion.

Laugh if you will when they heehaw
But know that they are crying
When they make that noise that sounds like something
Between a squawking water pump and a foghorn.

And when I hear them sobbing
I suddenly notice their sweet eyes and ridiculous ears
And their naive bodies that look as though they never grew up
But stayed children, as in fact they are;
And being misunderstood as children are
They are forced to walk up mountains
With men and bundles on their backs.

Somehow I am glad that they do not submit without a protest
But as their masters are of the deafest
The wails are never heard.

I am sure that donkeys know what life should be
But, alas, they do not own their bodies;
And if they had their own way, I am sure
That they would sit in a field of flowers
Kissing each other, and maybe
They would even invite us to join them.

For they never let us forget that they know
(As everyone knows who stays as sweet as children)

That there is a far better way to spend time;
You can be sure of that when they stop in their tracks
And honk and honk and honk.

And if I tried to explain to them
Why work is not only necessary but good,
I am afraid that they would never understand
And kick me with their back legs
As commentary on my wisdom.

So they remain unhappy and sob
And their masters who are equally convinced of being right
Beat them and hear nothing.

Goats

Our insides are not awfully different:
Like a tight sweater the skin pulls over the head;
A slit, and the entrails bulge,
Quite clean! I had imagined them bloody.
And how familiar their appearance:
Sausages never disgusted us before
So why should they now in the raw?

Not at all imagining themselves in the nibbled-at position,
A chicken pecks cozily at lean
And a cat chews a piece of fat.

Of course, by now there is no resemblance anymore
To a goat; more like a meat market:
The behind has turned into steaks
And all the other parts now have culinary names.
The gross butcher with small eyes and a stupid forehead
Starts hosing away the pools of blood,
And the expression on his face slowly changes
From Eternal Destroyer to haggling merchant.

Now the buyers in procession march
Joyfully to market
As they never do when relatives die,
For they know it would be ridiculous,

Even though unskinned he looks like us,
To mourn a goat.

And besides there is nothing to mourn;
Certainly not his death
While he cooks in peace in various kitchens,
Nor his life when he leapt from rock to rock.
And then he ba-a-a-d and died:
So let us be as joyful as he was,
Eating our goat stew,
Making the movement of dancing and the noise of singing,
Taking each others' bodies in our arms
And then filing simply off to bed.

THOMAS MCGRATH

McGrath's third wife, Eugenia Johnson, was a Greek-American. They were married in 1960, when he had just begun teaching again after the blacklist years. His sympathies for Greek culture really came to the fore, however, when he was able to live in Greece during 1967–68. The advent of the Junta and his increasing sense of the horror of military dictatorship in Greece only confirmed McGrath in his leftist convictions. Living on Paros and Skyros, he enjoyed a time of idyllic retreat from teaching responsibilities and was buffered from some of the turmoil in other parts of the country. But he was deeply aware of the sufferings of Greeks, as he would demonstrate in such poems as "You, Yannis Ritsos," "A Homecoming for Odysseus," and "Mediterranean."

Mike Hazard

It was also in Greece that he wrote portions of Part Two of *Letter to An Imaginary Friend* (1962). In a sense, his renewed education in the layered traditions of Greece allowed him to find an equivalence in North America. The heroes of Greek mythology could be compared to Crazy Horse, allowing McGrath to express the timelessness of all struggles for human dignity. Mythological structures of Europe could be compared to such Native American traditions as those he found in Frank Waters' *The Book of the Hopi*. Greece well may have given McGrath the perspective he needed to move his long poem beyond autobiography and toward its larger visionary schemata.

David Mason

from "Letter to an Imaginary Friend"

Part Two

I

1.   _____ coils in my ear like song...
                                        the dawn wind riding
Out of the black sea, knocks at my shutters. Cockcrow.
Before cockcrow: the iron poet striding over
This village where the horses sleep on the roofs, where now a lone
Rooster rasps the beak of his song on the crumbling tiles.

Skyros.
     In the false light before sunup.
I wait while the breeze,
Or a ghost, calls at the shutters.
                    Beyond the window the wild
Salt north forty of wind and water, the loud, galloping
White-maned mustangs of the cold ungovernable sea...

Honeysuckle, lavender, oleander, osiers, olive trees, acanthus—
All leafsplit, seedshaken, buckling under the drive
Of the living orient red wind
               constant abrasive
North Dakota
       is everywhere.
              This town where Theseus sleeps on his hill—
Dead like Crazy Horse.
           This poverty.
               This dialectic of money—

Dakota is everywhere.
         A condition.
             And I am only a device of memory
To call forth into this Present the flowering dead and the living
To enter the labyrinth and blaze the trail for the enduring journey
Toward the round dance and commune of light...
                     to dive through the night of rock
(In which the statues of heroes sleep) beyond history to Origin
To build the Legend where all journeys are one
                where Identity
Exists
     where speech becomes song...

         First bird sound now...
This morning Lambrakis overthrew the government in ghost-ridden Athens
Having that power of the dead out of which all life proceeds...
Genya smiles in her sleep. The arch of her foot is darkened
With the salt of the ancient sea and the oil of a bad century...
The light sharpens.
      The wind lifts.
         The iron poet

Strides out of the night and the instant world begins
Outside this window.

World where the rebels fall under
The Socratic tricycles of NATO gangsters, are plugged in the heart
By intercontinental ballistic musical moments mechanical
Pianos loaded with the short-fuse scrap iron of Missouri waltzes, guided
Missiles of presidential rocking chairs timed to explode on contact...
Texas fraternal barbecues: "Bring your own nigger or be one."

(And, of a mountain of wild thyme, its thunderous honey.)

The sea builds instantaneous lace which rots in full motion—
One-second halflife—just beyond this window.

Full light.
Cicadas.

A donkey brays on the citadel.

The world,

perfect
And terrible.

Sun in Gemini.

New moon at summer solstice
Perfect.

All changed and nothing changed and all to be changed.
I want the enduring rock, but the rock shifts, the wind
Lifts, Hell's always handy, you may enter the labyrinth anywhere
Beyond the window.

Where now the first fisherman goes out:
To the mother sea, to mine for the small fish and the big—
The hours and minutes of her circular heart—to dig in the turquoise
Galleries of her tides and diamond-studded lobsters with their eyes of
    anthracite...
Where his partner, the Hanged Man,

strangled in nets of poverty...

last night...
Last night. This morning. The rock and the wind.

North Dakota *is*
Everywhere.

2. "_____ seems like it was right here somewhere...
                                        place where you git out—
Hey there, resurrection man! ghost haunter, crazy damn poet,
What do you do now kid?"
                        (Voices from sleep, from death, from
The demoniacal dream called living.)
                        —I'm here to bring you
Into the light of speech, the insurrectionary powwow
Of the dynamite men and the doomsday spielers, to sing you
Home from the night.
                Night of America.
                        Gather you
At my million-watt spiritlamp, to lead you forward forever, to conquer
The past and the future...

                "Well just a doggoned minute now,
Whilst I gits my possibles sack, my soogans, my—"
                                —Heavy,
Heavy the weight of these choice souls on my sun-barked shoulder, heavy
The dark of the deep rock of the past, the coded legend
In the discontinuous strata where every voice exists—
Simultaneous recall: stone where the living flower leaps
From the angry bones of Precambrian dead.
                                Heavy the weight
Of Jim, of Jack, of my father, of Cal, of Lambrakis, Grimau,
Hiroshima, Cuba, Jackson...
                        heavy the weight of my dead
And the terrible weight of the living.

                "It's dark down here, man—
This slippery black—can't keep footin'—like climbin'
A greased pole, man—"
                And always, as I go forward,
And older I hear behind me, intolerable, the ghostlike footsteps—
Jimmy perhaps; or Jack; my father; Cal; Mac maybe—
The dead and the living—and to turn back toward them—that loved past—
Would be to offer my body to the loud crows and the crass
Lewd jackals of time and money, the academy of dream-scalpers, the mad

Congressional Committees on Fame, to be put on a crisscross for not
    wearing
The alien smell of the death they love
                         —they'd cram my bonnet
With a Presidential sonnet: they'd find my corpse worth stuffing
With the strontium 90 of tame praise, the First Lady to flay me
For mounting in the glass house of an official anthology...
                                        catafalques
Of bourgeois sensibility
              —Box A to Box Z...
                         And my body to suffer
(As my soul) dismemberment...
                    transmemberment...
                         my head
                              singing
                                   go down
The dark river...
            necessary—
               not to turn back.

"_____ and seems like it was right here someplace—place you git out..."
"Stick beans in your nose and you cain't smell honey." (Peets talking)
"Ain't no grab irons a man can lay hand to. *I tell you it's* DARK
DOWN HERE, MAN!
              slippery dark
                    can't see
                         I tell you it's hell—"

We must walk up out of this dark using what charms we have.
Hell's everywhere, this only seems like hell, take my hand,
It is only required to open your eyes—
                      see
                         there's
The land as it was
            these poor
                 the Indian graveyard
                       the coulee
The quaking aspens Genya and I planed last spring

At the old farmhouse.
                Unchanged and changed.
                                I tell you millions
Are moving,
        Pentagon marchers!
                       Prague May Day locomotives
With flowers in their teeth!
                     And now the red ball is hammering in—
Spot an empty! Grab an armful of rods!
                     I'll take you
In the final direction...
            Only:
                open your eyes...
But it's hard, hard, man.
            I'm standing *here,* naked
As a studhorse in a rhubarb patch
                  waiting
                    waiting
                      and here—
Around me
        trouble built for small boys and crazy men!
For my purpose (as I keep saying) is nothing less
Than the interposing of a fence of ghosts (living and dead)
Between the atomic sewing machines of bourgeois ideology
(Net where we strangle) and the Naked Man of the Round Dance...
"To perform instantaneous insurrectionary lobotomies for removing
The man-eating spinning wheels from the heads of our native capitalists."
To elaborate the iconic dynamite of the authentic class struggle
In other words to change the world
                —Nothing less.
                   It's hard and I'm
Scared...

The beginning is right here:
                ON THIS PAGE.
Outside the window are all the materials.
                  But I am waiting
For the colored stone...
            for the ghosts to come out of the night...

And now the village sleeps.
                        A heavy static,
                                        golden
Like the honey of lovesick buzz saws clots in the steepy light
And the tall and aureate oak of the august noon-high sun
Crumbles.
            That pollen.
                        Seeding the air...
                                        The cicadas (tzinzaras)
Are machining the sunlight in their chattering mills
                                        kind of Morse code

With a terrible signal-to-noise ratio—is it information
Comes through all that clatter or a mere random conformity
To a known Code?
                Minimax
                        bobbery
                                palaver
                                        —you can reduce shortfall
Only so much—finally...
                        it is necessary to act.
                                        Even
When the information is incomplete...
                                —That's all right:
I'll cut for a sign—and don't leave the gate open
                                        I'll
Catch my own snipes.
                        The village is *not* asleep, it is only
Siesta...

        A poor fisherman hanged in a net
Puts all heaven in a sweat...
                        The ratio of signal
To noise improves. I read you loud and clear. Over.

"—get out in the stream and *sing.*
                        It's a branch assignment,
                                        a job
For the revolutionary fraction in the Amalgamated Union of False
        Magicians,

Kind of boring, from within..."
                          Insurrectionary

                                    ancestral voices...
                                              —coming now—
Ghosts wreathed with invincible wampum—
                                    "Hey buddy
What you doing there in the dark?"
                          —How should I know?
                                          What I'm doing
Ain't nobody
          nowhere
                    never
                done before.

                        ⬛🔲🔲🔲🔲🔲🔲⬛

ROBERT LAX

When I left New York for Greece I had hoped only to find a quiet place to live for a while and write some poems. Quiet and inexpensive. If I

could have found an uninhabited island where I could forage for myself, I think I'd have gone there. I did not come looking for people or for nature, much less for history, just for quiet. I thought I needed it for my work, as a photographer needs a darkroom.

Quiet? A place to get away from people? Bright light, loud noises, and a constant presence of people (and of birds, goats, fish) is more the style. You are never alone in Greece. Someone is always with you, right with you or watching from across the hill: watching, listening, never sleeping, gathering data for a fund that has been growing for the past several thousand years, watching any flick of variation in patterns already known of human behavior. Wherever you live in Greece, whatever you do, wherever you

sleep, you are doing it on a brightly lighted stage. Each day is judgment day (from *Journal C/Tagebuch C,* Zurich: Pendo, 1990).

Why in Greece: because I feel that the landscape here is properly classical, properly stripped of all that is not essential, all that is not universal. It is ready-made for abstraction and for concrete, exact, particular abstraction.... I...know the language well enough to converse with people at almost every level of society, including the level that most interests me on this island: that of the fishermen and sponge divers. These are people, mostly unlettered, and who, even though they have sometimes traveled widely in terms of miles in the modern world, are really in mind much like the ancient Dorians, their forebears, neither simple nor unimaginably complex, but interesting in their response to [things], and in their responses to a modern man of the cities. But I am not here as an anthropologist, but as a poet and whatever in the daily life here feeds my spirit, feeds me more particularly as a poet (from "description of project," *The ABC's of Robert Lax,* 1999).

Shepherd's Calendar

1.

move	move	rocks	move
ment	ment	like	ment
of	of	sheep	of
sheep	sheep		rocks
move	move	sheep	move
ment	ment	like	ment
of	of	rocks	of
rocks	rocks		rocks

2.

the	the
sheep's	bell's
bell	tongue
the	the
sheep's	sheep's
tongue	tongue
the	the
sheep's	sheep's
bell	tongue
the	the
bell's	bell's
tongue	tongue

3.

the	the
sheep	boy
eats	waits
the	the
boy	sheep
waits	eats
the	the
sheep	boy
eat	waits
the	the
boy	sheep
waits	eat

4.

sheep	boy
wan	throws
ders	stones
boy	sheep
throws	wan
stone	der
sheep	sheep
wan	wan
der	ders
boy	boy
throws	throws
stones	stone

5.

bleat	bleat
lamb	sheep
bleat	bleat
sheep	lamb
sheep	sheep
eats	eat
sheep	sheep
eat	eats

6.

```
drift          sink
shad           sun
ow

drift          drift
sheep          shad
               ow

drift          sink
shad           sun
ow

drift          drift
sheep          sheep
```

The Harbor

the v's & w's in
the harbor

waves & wave
troughs

black wild waves
& yellow lights

nervous fretful
sea

unwilling to
talk

unwilling to
keep silent

waves pursued
by waves

glance back
over shoulder

restless sleepers
of the broad black
sea

all night they
talk

all night
they shout

calling hoarsely
one over the other

uttering their
manifold complaint

no one waits
answer

speaks & respeaks
the anguish of
his heart

quiet as a garden

evening on the island

in all the compounds

melancholy thinkers

eyes of a middle dis-
tance on the floor

no speech: lips
utter words

but heart

is silent

_____

antigone is
unappeased

the furies & every
vengeance still
pursues

electra mourns

cassandra pro
phecies

(times change, but
ancient voices
fill the air)

_____

blood guilt
is blood guilt

blood begets
blood

the gods are
unappeased

by human
justice

_____

all the ancient
battles

fought
refought

all the ancient
oracles

respoken

-----

impassive as
the statue's
brow

the melancholy
thinker's

lips speak
but are as
quiet as
stone

what says the
heart
the dark heart
darkly knows

what says the
sea

the black wave
tells the
sky

Byzantine Faces

i won't believe
i'm really
alive

until i'm gladder
to be alive
here now
than to have
been alive
there then

living in greece
i may be
thinking
i am, was,
alive there
then

some byzantine
time
some classical
time

why think
that good?

i should
know better
yes, but i keep
remembering
a light in the
eyes of certain
figures in
frescoes

certain figures
in mosaics

that made
me wish

i think good
any time except
the eighteenth
century

(not too bad)

the nineteenth
century

(bad enough)

or the twentieth

really, i'm
glad to be
alive in the
twentieth

not only glad
to be just
alive

but even to
be alive
just now
right now

eternally
alive
eternally
infinitely
joyous
& penetrating

(warm with
the warmth
of life
exploding,
even, with

I was living
then

as though
living then

were to
live

forever

some life
some liveliness
in the eye
that seemed
eternal

is it
that see
ing them
in some
mu
se
um

seeing
them still
preserved
still
living

made me
envy
their
state

?

not
sure

the joy
of life)

yet there
forever

am
not
sure
either,
that it
was envy
they gave
me, but
rather a
life

a spark
of living
to keep
alive

[untitled]

which
is
bet
ter

to
be
here
now

or
to
be
there
then
?
- - - - -

the
on
ly
way
to
be

is
to
be
here
now

- - - - -

the
way
to
be
here
now

is
to
be
there
now

- - - - -

to
be
here
now

(there
is
no
there

there
is
no
then)

the
on
ly
way
to
be
(there
then)

is
to
be
here
now

the
way
to
be
there
now

is
to
be
here
now

the
on
ly
way
to
be

is
to
be
now

- - - - -

the
on
ly
there

there
is

is
here

- - - - -

here
on
this
spot

here
on
this
is
land

here
in
this
sea

here
on
this
earth
- - - - -

the
on
ly
place
to
be

is
to
be
here

but
here
has
broad
di
men
sions

here
&
now

here
in
this
sys
tem

here
in
this
un
i
verse

here
in
the
mind
of
God

all
heres
are
here

all
thens
are
now

PHILIP RAMP

It almost goes without saying that Greece has had an enormous and undoubtedly beneficial effect on my poetry, first of all because ninety percent of my work has been writ-ten during my thirty-eight years in Greece. I have acquired a sense of living history I probably never would have gained in the United States. Clearly modern and ancient Greece share so many aspects that nothing in the country has died so much as been transformed. There is an ongoing merging and breaking apart, a constant process of reinte-gration and dissolution. If there are echoes of other poets in my work, then they are from Karouzos rather than Stevens, Ritsos rather than Roethke. Whether my poems are connected to Greek themes, child-hood memories, or any other themes I'm drawn to, there is a more abstract sense of the present in my work than there would have been, or could have been, had I remained in the States. But then Greece is the navel of the world after all. The Muses are from here. What more can a poet ask for?

Don Schofield

Rock

The walls of a medieval garrison still bear the scars of brigands
and higher up an even older temple wears other marks
vague and yet as indelible as time, in honor, you might say
of the more enduring but still declining hills.
Anyway, the hills camouflage the ruins, the ruins the hills.

If you pull back, shift thought's all-too-easy focus from eternity
then all there is, it seems, is rock:
rock tumbling headlong and unstoppable, plunging to the sea
slowed not at all by the fable power of that sea
soothed of course by aeons of unrelenting liquid death
but not softened, still rock and going down and down
till it breaks through the limits of the sea
to stroke the molten stony sap that drives the earth.

Focus once again and the sap is there cooled and hardened all around you
in the stony brush and rocky flowers
that clog what at first seem bare and inhospitable ravines,
impervious to the bullets of the rain or the sun's incandescent bore.
Then look up higher next to the temple and the garrison
and between the huts and folds concealed among the hills:
there's the old olive tree, the disguised organic engine of the stone
built to run on that sap and convert it into nutrient
to feed its green and silver leaves on a food that will not fail
forcing plump that black fruit whose endurance has come to mean prevail.

A Temple

The temple over there is doing rather well I think,
a small, neat pile, all its very own
and as the stand of pine that frames it dwindles
it's forced to maintain increasingly alone
whatever ambience one might attribute to that place—
each year's postcards show a boost in unassisted dignity.
If you wait long enough, or are lucky,
you'll still find a moon to grace
the sheen of its silvery fever
though the moon's been lessened by other light
and the fever may break into a simpler, sicklier hue.

But why dwell on these abiding depredations?
As I said, the temple is doing rather well
and while some, well maybe many,
are dismissive of such meager ruins
I must say I am not—
not that I am disinclined to what's ancient and intact
but in fact these faint configurations tell me more:

like for how long no one cared
(less than scorn, more than neglect)
yet somehow it held on to enough of the unqualified
to insure it would endure
enough perhaps to engender adequate uncertainties
in those who once thought to build,
but then did not, their dwellings of its stony mystery.
It had a while and used it well
and now, I think, it's got it right.
It's earned all the praise it gets and more
To me it now looks like the old god
It was supposed to stand in for should look:
I mean, like some grand memory you are forgetting
but haven't yet forgot.

Becky Dennison Sakellariou

I believe I am deeply affected by my environment, no matter where or what it may be. My perceptions, my consciousness, my vision all are very directly connected to the physical, human, and spiritual worlds around me. Because my writing responds to these relationships, it follows that the Greek "world," in all its components, is integral to what and how I write. It also follows that the New England "world" also permeates my writing, since it framed and defined my first perceptions and my early experiences. Perhaps I could say that the extreme differences between the world of my childhood in the northeastern corner of the United States and that of my adulthood in Mediterranean/Balkan Greece have created a continuing tension in my engagement in the world and thus in my poetry. I believe that this tension resonates for me specifically through the sounds and "feeling" of language and the colors, textures, and shapes of landscape and that my poetry speaks to this aspect of my life.

Jan Friar

Breathing

At the olive press this morning, I leaned
my face against the iron grid above the great
steel blades grinding the olives through
the long bin, wet mottled green dough
that would pour silky oil out the final
thin tube, where the smell was the smell
of sour bread made from earth,
from well water, from women squatting

on the hard ground, fingers flying, gathering
the fallen olives under the trees, compact bodies
moving in the tall grasses, finding the fat purpled
fruit, murmuring of Maria and her hard man,
Panagiota's difficult pregnancy, Lenio wanting
to leave the village, Stellio driving too fast,
the strange summer rains that ruined the grape
harvest. The men perch high in the trees, whapping
the branches with long gnarled sticks kept
in the corners of the shed, the olives pour down
like hail onto the great crackling sheets
of plastic wrapped around the tree base.
I press my face again to the grid and breathe in
the smoky odor like wet cat fur, slept-in
bedclothes, rotting leaves. I wish my hands
down into the dark must, pushing them
in up to the elbows, sliding the hot mass
through my fingers, the pungent steam
rising, the fermenting fragments of pits
and skin coating my hands, the smell rolling
on and on, flowing over the fertile chalice of the earth.

I Would Like to Write Poems

I would like to write poems
in Greek and read them

to you, my tongue lifting
the sibilant lisp of the *s*,

the watery *r* rippling
across the roof

of my mouth, the *p*
that settles on the inside

of my lower lip. You wouldn't
understand, but you would hear

words like *psomi* and *aftonomia,*
monopati and *parathiro,*

and you would close your eyes
and begin to see the early

light, white and dry,
the long loops of grapes

woven between leaves shaped
like your hands. You would smell

sour bread and hard worked
bodies, *rigani* and night

blooming jasmine. You might
even hear old voices telling

far tales of valor
and muskets, men with huge mustaches

and their dusky women whose names
were never spoken.

BARRY TAGRIN

It can be fairly said that I was born in Greece, if we use consciousness as a measure instead of place and time. I arrived in Rhodos in 1969 and in the

ancient maze-like streets of Lindos met Jack Gilbert and Linda Gregg on a brilliant moonlit night. It was a fortuitous occurrence, because through them I was able to unravel the aspects of classical Greek mythology and literature and take a step up into a brighter, more solid world. Heroic archetypes and emotional and romantic patterns came into focus; the concept of Beauty as it was invented by the Greeks became a reality rather than an idea. Later, there were the wonderful years of my marriage to Karen on Santorini and Paros where the Cycladic landscapes formed not only the backdrop of my lyrical poems, but also the very spiritual center of my own equilibrium. Greece has been more than an influence; it was, and is, partner to my poetry. The land itself, caretaker. Certainly, I belong nowhere else, and in my home on the mountain I feel secretly holy, because I built the house by hand from the stones beneath its base, just the way my neighbor, Yorgo, taught me. Socratic, and clear.

Returning to Greece

For a few days I was alone.
It was cold and gray, I spoke to
the mountain.

In my solitude I discovered the intensity
of my lies. The deception I had dressed in

to keep the two
women I loved.

My heart also was in bed with this duplicity.
It would not allow in the winter light
either of the women to defeat the other.

So it is true that worlds collide and there is damage.
And nothing is the same afterwards. Beauty
and sadness make one.

The melancholy leaves of the weeping trees.
And walking along the terraces I built.
Greece being torn apart.

Many things ruined, as others are born.
And we cannot, either of my selves, rest
with the other.

We just strike out at a man divided.
While sweet things, like breakfast and rain,
are spoiled by doubt.

Sorrow Flying Hard

I am so tired of my habits. My heart
is stretched out and biting into itself.
Life is no longer a dream moving across the island.

I look at my neighbor working in the dirt at eighty-five,
making the onions and the tomatoes
for his last summer.

I love my son and my grandson.
I don't love abandoning Karen,
and my marriage.

Occasionally I go into the rabbits and the almonds,
to try and keep my past alive,
as I work at closeness with Yuko.

I fear becoming a river bottom, so dry
with debris atop, languishing
in the summer heat.

All that radical inattention
I grew up with. And no one
to blame.

BILL MAYER

I was born and raised in one of the endless suburbs of Los Angeles.
Though I would not wish to give the impression that L.A. was an American version of Dickensian squa-
lor, it did not particularly
stimulate the life of the spirit.
That life I had to find through
books. Greece was introduced to
me first through the writings of
Richard Halliburton, an adven-
turer of the twenties and thirties
who wrote the sort of books that
enabled a sensitive boy to clamber out of the prosaic world and
let his imagination go wild. *Glori-
ous Adventure* was Halliburton's
romantic (and somewhat comic)
retracing of the wanderings of
Odysseus. It was exactly the sort
of thing I needed, and I find I can
still read the book with pleasure

Jan Clark

(though wincing at some of his social views). Later, Greece came alive
when I was reading Nikos Kazantzakis, and eventually when I met both
his wife and Kimon Friar, one of his first translators. What I wanted was
magic, and Greece gave that. The myths burned into my brain; the sculpture and architecture were more beautiful than anything I had ever seen;
and the plays and poetry were harsh and true. Lawrence Durrell writes
somewhere that, whereas Italy is a supremely civilized land, something
about the nature of Greece is wild and undomesticated. Greece forces
you, he wrote, to confront yourself.

In the late winter of 1980, my companion and I took a boat from
Brindisi to Corfu. It was a wild and stormy night ride; the Ionian waves
smashed into the ferry. There were great troughs, and I could see
through the porthole a mountain of water high above me. Almost everyone was sick. The stewards had handed out plastic containers with tops,
which, half-full, scrabbled across the lower decks as if under their own
power. The smell was dreadful. Sometime very early in the morning the
storm abated. Sleep being impossible, I went up on deck and looked

through the cold gloom for my first sight of Greece. After almost an hour I saw something darker than the dark around. As the light grew and the clouds began to break up, first the form of the mountain of Corfu appeared, then the snow-covered peaks of Albania just across the strait. I felt like Odysseus coming home.

Most of that year we lived on the island of Paros in a falling-down Venetian villa about five miles from the main town, Paroikia. It had two bedrooms, a kitchen, and an outhouse. There was also a private chapel with a marble lintel dating from 1659. Beside the house was a stream that could be diverted into a cistern. It served as a sort of underwater refrigerator, especially useful for chilling the local *retsina*. I'd walk into town about twice a week, through Butterfly Valley just above us, over the mountain, past the nunnery, past a few chapels, and down the donkey track into town.

Living on the island was difficult, sometimes painful, but always marvelous. On the boat leaving the island, with tears in our eyes, we swore we'd be back, and soon. My companion returned a couple of years later and lives there still with her Greek husband. I have not yet returned. But the spirit of the place still informs my life and work. On my desk is a small wine bottle about half-full with water I took from the Castalian Fountain at Delphi. Above it on the wall is a sprig of laurel from the only laurel tree I could find close to the spring. It must be the one, or a descendant of the one, that Apollo planted and made sacred. With these close by I write my poems.

Neither Memory nor Nostalgia

Two lives live in me
            beating with my heart beating
                        though not together
                                    apart
                                    and though the afternoon
                                        sun shines on both
                        equally
Tiny boats on the distant water going nowhere
            red sail   yellow sail   blue sail
And even though a girl in a simple shift should come to me and loosen her belt
though there were perfumes   also
                in the protected waters
People want or need things.
They call. I help them. I am busy
                                            forgetting
                                            And though the
                                                god emerges

naked, dripping, the sheen on the wet, brown skin blinding
and do you dare recognize   or else
                                        Two lives that do not love each other

We would walk down the hill along the ancient track to the little pier, and take
the tiny caïque across to the next island. Then go past the town to the north end
and the beach. The water was very shallow there. We continued across the little
strait, holding our things above our heads in the deepest part, and then up onto
the shore of the next islet. Which was uninhabited, though there were ancient
threshing circles and large, crude shards everywhere. The last island was two
hundred feet away and you could walk that easily, the water being no more than
two feet deep. On it we found a small private beach, and put our things down
and swam naked under the Aegean sun. I remember once being stung by
something in the water, perhaps a ray, which was very painful. I do not remember
if we made love there. I only remember
that there was no death
                    that the figs and melons and cucumbers we carried with us
were our hearts beating
the work done on the weekdays, the work inside, this work that I make

                              I did not do this to make a career.
But if the sails were lifted, and bellying out, and caught the light winds
and moved towards me
would I put my things down
and get up and go with them
Is it age   that prevents   or does it prevent
could I do it
could I

20

Our life was easy.
We lacked nothing. Lived here,
learned. We spent our time
with one desire: to say the simplest things
to each other, without guile.
But this was not easy at all.
I tell you, our life was hard.
So sweet and painful this island was,
soft on the Aegean.
The ships passed by.

We lay on the bed pretending.
We were lonely, finally.
Sad. Circled each other
with caution. We left nothing.

After

I no longer remember the daily clarity
of living in Greece, except that it was clear.
But what, for instance, did we talk about
those warm evenings when the sun slipped
behind the plane trees and we began to prepare dinner?
And later, when there was little to read and we were left
to each other in the high ceilinged rooms;
that must be where we failed.
I do remember the silence.
It would have taken more courage than we had to resist it.
But to have made a kind of music, not once,
not just at the beginning—how much clarity,
how much perseverance would it have taken?

RACHEL HADAS

Greece—its language, landscape, culture—is doubly important in my work. No, make that triply. Or better, fourfold. Fivefold.

First: As a Classics major, I studied Greek literature in college and went to Greece in part to find the country behind the words. Second: When I arrived in Greece, the beauty of the landscape (particularly at that time in Samos, where I lived for several years) eclipsed my purely literary acquaintance with the place. Third: When you live somewhere and form human connections, those in turn become the foreground for which the sea, the mountains, the islands form a backdrop. Fourth: Living in Greece and learning Modern Greek, which sucked strength from, even as it depleted, my Ancient Greek, added a new dimension to my sense of what Greece was and is. Fifth: Living in Greece largely on an island, away from literary connections, I turned with all the more ardor to the American poets then living in Athens whom I intermittently saw a great deal of: James Merrill, Chester Kallman, and Alan Ansen, among others. A conversation with Alan in those days taught me more about literature (particularly the poetry of Auden) than I had picked up at Harvard; a casual but penetrating comment from Jimmy Merrill on a draft poem was worth hours of workshop discussion. The workshops in fact came later when I went back to school (I earned an M.A. in Poetry from the Hopkins Writing Seminars in 1977). When I studied poetry and later comparative literature, it was, as it were, with Greece under my belt. The literature, the language, the people, the landscape: Perhaps these are in turn now the background for other concerns and themes, but they remain intrinsic to my work. Besides, you never know with poetry when the background will come forward, or the foreground will slink into the distance.

Roy Groething

69

A Copy of Ariel

Not only is the bookmark still in "Poppies in July,"
but I can smell the mildew still—a seamold's
rich and acrid pale-brown sour tang.
Or is it that the book enfolds a world
bleary but flowering with possibilities?
Each morning I gazed at the milky sea
and it was always morning. It was morning
when, making one more effort to efface
the person I had always been, I thought
"Why not translate 'Poppies in July'
into Greek?" And it was also morning
when my first original Greek poem
was born of gazing. But Plath's poppies first.
I recall those little bloodied skirts,
the thin as paper dry and bloodied lips,
translucent delicacies, onion skins,
and the skeptical question "*Do* you do no harm?"
(my italics) which could be translated
rather than answered.

                          As for my own poem,
it never got beyond the first two lines:
Phortoma gaidouria kai karpousa!
Phtasane ta kaikia ap'ta nisa.
("Cargo of donkeys and watermelons!
The fishing boats have arrived from the islands.")

The poem was no more than a transparent
container for four juicy neuter plurals
(donkeys, watermelons. caiques, islands)—
an embryonic grammar beyond which
I failed to move. I had no more to say.
No human face looked back at me. A life,
motives—illegible. What I still can see
is the horizon, pallid amulet
beckoning above the shimmer of gray sea;
and sense, even now, my dim determination
to hold onto what could in any case
never be lost. So that those ghostly poppies
and smell of paper mildewing in mist—

smell edible, perishable as meat—
both open vistas, far, symmetrical;
whereas the donkeys (hoisted with a crane
onto the *limani*) or the glistening
bulbous melons bounding in the hull,
naked of meaning but for brilliant outlines,
were called back into being only through
the rules of grammar and my meager Greek
word hoard—called back, though, as genuine
visions, even if the haze through which they shone
yielded to each morning's arrow: sun.

Rag Rug

It has arrived at last—the long rag rug
   multiply folded. On top, one alien hair.
      I put my face to the folds and smell despair
         palpable as salt air
      in all those rooms and houses, small and smug—
enclosures I passed through on my way where?

Whoever did the weaving appears old
   in my mind's eye. I can't make out her face,
      can only conjure up the faintest trace
         of an abstracted grace,
      clack of the loom. Does she know they'll be sold,
these precious things, in some unheard-of place?

I perch her on a hill, precariously
   beyond the reach of the waves' daily boom.
      Sun blazes overhead, but her dim room
         (no bigger than the loom)
      is proof against the violence of the sky.
From it I further spin what I once called home:

Endless horizons fading into haze,
   the mornings dawn came up so rosy-clear;
      snails in the garden, sheep bells everywhere,
         the brightness of the air,
      terraces, valleys organizing space
and time's cessation. So this package here

I'm now unwrapping, in New York, today
 (rugs like rainbows, woven with a grace
  my strands of language barely can express;
   dishrags of dailiness
  dispersed and recombined and freshly gay)
comes to me imbued with images,

slowly and faithfully across the water,
 across the world. It represents a time
  I myself snipped and recombined as rhyme
   as soon as I went home,
  if that is where I am. These rugs recover
the sense of stepping twice into a single river.

Last Trip to Greece

I had the labels ready with their essence:
Add water, serve. Light, language, beauty, sea,
body, etcetera, etcetera. Time.
In honesty I need to change the tune:
queasiness, boredom, and misogyny.
Forget the little table by the sea
under an awning. Stupefied by sun,
we were to have sat musing over dreams
dreamed in the shuttered twilight of siestas.
No. There was sitting, though—sitting and waiting.
Minutes ticked by. The sluggish month of June
little by little shifted its big bulk,
morning to evening, dawn to afternoon,
till it was time to climb back on the plane.

The very language was to have been a spell
I'd left half woven, alien, magical,
testing the murky waters with my tongue...
Ha! I remembered everything too well.
Words meant the culture that they dragged along.
I entered it each time I acquiesced
to vowels and consonants and all the rest.
The language had three genders, it was true,
but only one that mattered. What was new
was how I saw this world as one of men.

The energy was men's, men's was the joy:
the sun-dark muscles at the soccer match
matched the colossal kouros' marble thigh,
the only thing of beauty in Vathy—

skillfully rendered, lovingly observed,
alert and timeless in its stony way.
But these were partial pleasures—half a world.
Where was the realm of women? Where was I?
Could all we weaker vessels be boiled down
to that one expedition to the convent?
We rose so early sun and moon still shared the sky
to climb the mountain, find the nuns halfway
to heaven, but beyond the reach of time,
of energy clocked by sinew or by speed.
With their cracked bells, devotions, goats, and hens,
their sanctuary of bees and running water,
their milk and ouzo offered thirsty travelers,
do they have all of paradise they need?

I wasn't made to live in paradise.
And I'd this misconception about time.
The precious element became a baggy
garment in whose folds I nearly smothered,
however fervently I'd dreamed of it
before I put it on. For too much time
is like a swirling cloak without an opening.
You cannot use your arms to work, you almost
go down like Agamemnon in the bath
speared by his furious consort Clytemnestra,
that queen whose weapon bridged two worlds with blood—
and whom, although I thought I knew the myth,
I grew to be more sympathetic with.
Oh, everything had changed! Or was it simply me?

Idées reçues I'd readily affixed
to nature like a pair of rosy lenses
had somehow come undone. The gentle sheep bells
tinkling on Acrocorinth when I first
visited the place ten years ago
still tintinnabulated; but this time
what made the day was an enormous snake

sliding into a hole. He owned the place.
He—but why he? What sex are guardian serpents?
And who was I? Well, newly pregnant; queasy;
uneasy in the combat zone I kept
perceiving between what were now two worlds,
the fight a sudden struggle in my gut.
Oh god, how much I wanted to go home!

Urgency was the measure of regret
for what I'd had and seen and lost and learned;
of hope, as well, for what I was becoming,
for what I needed distance to make true.
Dreams meanwhile took on firm geometries:
one family member wedged into each corner,
the loaded silence palpable between them
as I took courage, made my brief announcement,
and shattered certain symmetries for good.
Forever. Change on both sides, in the middle;
change in my middle. I wasn't pedestaled,
entranced in a museum; nor did I float
dreamily above the pool of time.
All the old lineaments were ripe for change.

Island Noons

I

All day there's nothing to do but sprawl in the sun
reading of fountains, meadows, hills, and groves.
Nothing to do but float in a blue
fluid through which forgotten
words shoot up like bubbles.

And there that day when the great light of heaven
Burned at his lowest in the rolling year,
On the waste sand by the waste sea they closed

my eyes as I lie on the beach
to block the glare. I will a cloud to come,
mask the fierce zenith.
It does come. It subtracts

shadows from the water.
Distant baby islands
invisible before
surface clear through the caldron of haze
simmering in the south.
A point of lilac light
thrusts from behind the mountain.
A hint of wind: the ocean will be colder.

I tell myself I knew this change would come.
Even in paradise
there must be shades of weather.
But the cloud passes.
A shadow on the sand
makes me lift my head.
Dizzily I squint
at Ariadne. Knock-kneed, light behind her,
shyly she smiles hello, tries on a flipper.
Her eyes are blue. I have no words to give her.

I put the poet down and plunge away,
the secret greenwood seared and quenched
and hissing in salt water.
Habit makes me scan
the skyline as I float
for any uprights
except the masts of fishing boats.
Gently they rock at anchor.
At the shell-fanged stones of the prewar harbor
I cling, drip, count the houses
along Poseidon Street,
their shuttered windows blank as new green blackboards.
The number never comes out quite the same.

Even years later
it's not much easier
to tell the truth about the place,
not to speak of its prettiness
as of a painted screen.
But let me try to put the noons
together and stand back
now the long day is over.

Cowled in routine, buying my bread at the oven,
perhaps I think the place will never learn to read me.
Each day I wear demotic
and when I take the mask off what is there?
Numberless gem-bright stones
dull on the beach as I bend to touch them.
Ironies and omissions stop my mouth like sand.

Caressingly they said,
"Look how devoted! See, she follows him
everywhere, as far
as the ends of the earth, think of it—
even as far as here."
And I'd reply, "But it is beautiful,
I like it here." (In Greek, *it likes me here*.)

Village, I learned your words but not your music.
I had no melody worth the taking.
I wore an ineffectual disguise—
blue smock, plastic sandals—
but must have seemed enough a local woman
after a while for them to ask, "You haven't
forgotten your first language yet? You will?"

No books but what I'd bought or once had read—
like Tennyson still floating in my head.
No mirrors but the water and the sky.
No verticals except the granite mountain
to punctuate the landscape. Shuttered houses
huddled together—still in fear of pirates?
Two rooms. The secret fetters. The loud ocean.

As if to tear a pastel sketch in two,
pierce it through,
this shine and ruffle of the sun on water,
and touch the bedrock of ineffable
truth that is waiting in an ill-lit corner
or would be if—no, here there is no dimness.
Quench the sun, still this world is washed in light.

I squint to try to see.
Years squint back at me.
Eden, oasis, exile, island, desert—
if I don't choose a name
what will become of time?
Untrammeled days roll down the moving oar,
plop back into the sea.

Samian Morning, 1971

The gypsy loomed in the open door of morning,
bulky, unsmiling, her head wrapped in a scarf.
Her hand was out. She wanted something from me.

I don't remember whether I faced her fully.
Had I looked her straight in the eye and then beyond her,
I would have seen the Aegean like a frame.
If I had looked far enough over her right shoulder,
I would have seen Patmos lifting in a strip of light
from the horizon's lip. Over her left
shoulder I could have craned and seen Ionia.
But both these radiant regions were blocked off
not only by the figure in the doorway.

Where had she come from? Behind the house was a field.
Beyond this square green field—it was a wheatfield—
were a bent fig tree and a low stone wall
and a whitewashed hut like a gatehouse. Behind the wall
a road wound north away from the coast to the village.
She could have just walked up Poseidon Street
to ours, the last house in the row. But I think
she came around from the side, the back, the North.
I used to think the wind blew straight from Russia.
Turkey was left, the East,
and right and West was the great granite mountain.

My stinginess and resentment balanced by shame,
I gave the gypsy something I remember
probably only because she scowled and reproached me.
Whether she came back a second time
to try again, another woman with her,

is wavering conjecture. But I see all right
the thing I gave her: bright yellow, cashmere,
still with its Saks Fifth Avenue label,
a sweater someone had given me, no doubt,
for the same reason I tried to palm it off
on the gypsy, who rejected it with scorn.
The sweater was marred. A stain like a port wine birthmark
splotched the front. Who would wear such a thing?
Not I. Not she. I recall the botched transaction
but have to supply the shining of the sea,
brilliant backdrop to the piebald life
I must have turned back to after the gypsy, grumbling,
took herself away from the open door,
though I do not know if I turned to it with relief.

Donald Brees

I first went to Greece in the early 1970s. Linda Gregg had convinced me of the importance "to go where the gods still live," and a friend recommended Paros. I didn't know anyone on the island; it was winter and somehow I found an old remote farmhouse to rent for six dollars a month. There was no electricity in the countryside then; people rode donkeys or walked, living the way they had for generations. I spent my days next to a small stone window that looked out and down to the sea, reading Pound, Cavafy, Golding's translation of Ovid's *Metamorpheses* and what I had of Jack Gilbert's poetry. In the evenings, I'd go down to the village and sit with the men in the *kafeneion*. Then, late at night I'd start the long walk back up the valley on an ancient road under a map of the stars, sneaking past farms so as not to set off the dogs. Walking where Archilochus walked, the night sounds, the Aegean always in the distance, the wind, the loneliness—all that made the world magic. I have tried to render my experience into poems. I lived on other islands, but keep coming back to Paros. Someone once said, "The mountains are in the wrong place on the other islands."

Kalo Pedia

The three young communists aren't from the village.
When the Baba Nikolo comes in they motion for him to sit.
It's election week and the talk is politics.
When the old man tries to make a point, he's interrupted.
Finally he gives up, and with a laugh
tells them they are good men, but young.
They buy raki. It's time to finish him off.

The bearded one bends forward, coldly making his point.
The other two are almost shouting. The old man beams,
then he starts singing. Singing the old songs.
Sings and sings until his voice gives out.
Then he thanks everyone, insists on paying for everything,
and walks out into the night.

Kafeneion

In the early morning the old men sit out in front
facing the sun. Workers are stopping
for coffee. By ten, only a few men reading newspapers.
In the afternoon men come one at a time.
Play cards or backgammon. And nothing happens.
At night the talk is different. Politics
over ouzo and beer. Street repairs and garbage collection.
Yorgos starts picking up glasses.
At midnight men wander off into the night.
They know how to talk. How to listen.
How things get done. If someone calls Dimitri,
his wife says he's at the café.
But that's not really what she says.
She says, "He's working."

The Fox on Paros

The stones fall under foot.
The sky does not exist.
The sun is a hole in the eye of the fox.
At night the fox becomes so small
you can feel its breathing.
You know when its fur brushes your ankle.
You hear the screams of its food
becoming fox.

The Hermit at Piso Livadi

It was late winter, he had no money,
and somehow he'd talked himself into living
in an abandoned fishing village.
Days without speaking.

Two years since she's been in the café.
All the men are staring at her. She sits
near the one foreigner. They begin talking.
Someone sends ouzo to their table.

It was still dark when she drew a map for him.
"It's the farthest farm from the road.
I'll leave a lamp in the window.
If you come tonight, you've decided to stay."

The door opened, she had a brush in her hand.
"I heard the dogs." The room was full of steam.
A pot of water boiling on the stove.
"Put your clothes on the chair," she said pointing,
"I'm going to scrub you down."

JEFFREY CARSON

A newly married youth, I first came to Greece for half a year in 1965–66 for three reasons: first, because I was in love with classical art, literature,  and mythology; second, because I was infatuated with the words *Greek island;* and third, because I wanted somewhere to write the poetry I felt gathering. I returned to Greece in 1970, it seems permanently, because during my first stay I had felt as if the Aegean seascape and my developing inscape were one. For our first twelve years my wife and I lived in a simple, white country farmer's cottage with no electricity, no running water, no paved road nearby, no heat; it had leaky cane ceilings, a little garden, and was surrounded by wheatfields and vineyards. It commanded a splendid view of sea and sunset. Waking up, the first sound I heard was wavebeat and reflux, different every day, and when I went out I first looked at the movements in the bay below. Sea and rock and olive trees have meant to me what woods and running water meant to Wordsworth.

From the New York jazz of my youth, from Pindar's lines on the page that Hölderlin loved, from a line of Marvell and the forms of Herbert, from mad Pound and desperate Eliot and excitable Yeats, I started to build in the Aegean surf a nymphaîon where Keats could say Minos' cadenced words. Odysseus Elytis, whom I translated for twenty-five years, showed me how Law was a literal translator of sacred Chaos. I try to remember, *poesy* is Greek for *making*, and *icon* for *image*. With Greek light and the English language, I have sought to reach that horizon where Helios and Hades touch, and then to look back at the world as though through an icon brightly: that is, to be really here.

After Passover

Listen, Passover must have been over because the songbird cocks were singing and displaying and the hens were flying about with green twigs in their beaks.

And she was already outside still in her nightgown tending the roses in big earthen pots.

The birds kept singing and the roosters and donkeys too and goats were setting out from the stable.

The olive trees were flowing down to the sea and a trickle of water in the seasonal riverbed flowed through them; the canes were young, the broom not yet flowering.

The stones on the walls were octopus-gray but could change color if you looked at them hard.

The sea was seen to part aglitter and the way to all the islands was clear; the way to that island was clear, and not far, and the sunlight gleamed on the walls of water and on the way of water.

No, these are not shored memories.

Because the old days are the same as the new days when the sea is a certain color and when the lemon trees are flowering.

We'll save the sadness for later, we don't need it now.

Colossal Wind

You can't help but hear this colossal wind
Coming off the sea; it dwarfs the cypresses,
Wrecks clouds and anthills, piles stones
On beaches, wrapping them in weed.

Give thanks you're safe from shipwreck
And the weather report's delirium, when even
The ancient olive with its thick roots strains
For stature and the roofbeams of your cottage
Creak with effort and you know they'll hold.

The dog lies alert in the open garage,
The cats crouch nervously behind her,

Her long ears lie flat.
The electricity's out, the bike's knocked over,
A flowerpot's rolling.

                    Give thanks
You're safe from shipwreck when the colossal sea
And wind are swelling with reflux of eros
That hardly ever has itself in balance.

Tomatoes of Paros

Grow these tomatoes rightly
And they will be almost too sweet
But like a kiss
Leave your lips burning.

Paros Minor

Between Naxos and Mykonos I have disclosed
An island with a house for us and a garden
Watered by a spring named for a nymph,
And called it *Paros Minor.* Though it is small
We could not learn its secrets in a lifetime
Or weep enough for any of its woes
Or keep a daybook filled with all its flora
Or its migrating birds that stop to rest,
To drink, to eat the grasses' snails and insects.
There's shade for summer sun and walls for winter,
A room for shuttered thinking, and a small
Olive grove for strolling in at dusk.
Here pleasure turns to joy and lust to love,
Perplexity to verse, and daily sadness
To abstract thought or rhyme. I have disclosed
That fantasy of bookish humanists,
A lover's isle, whose lovely shape is close
On clear days in our blue Aegean straits.
                                        —*May 1993*

LAUREL MANTZARIS

To me, Greece is synonymous with the sea. I am lucky. I have some lovely kids—Greek kids—and a nice house a block away from the sea where I swim every day, summer and winter, hot or cold, rain or shine. The reality I find in the sea is so immediate, so impossible to shut out, so startling, so invigorating, that it more than makes up for the half-light I sometimes contend with on solid ground.

Cheryl Kozlow

Besides the obvious advantages of living in a place so full of natural beauty, vivacious people, and history, in Greece I have been able to pick and choose—see what I want to see, hear what I want to hear, and, to some extent, do what I want to do. The latter was pointed out by a Greek friend one day when I, still wet from an exhilarating winter swim and dressed in old sweats and rubber thongs, picked up my daughter from nursery school while the other mothers had made the chore an occasion to wear fashionable furs and leather. "You can paint your hair purple if you want to, and people will just accept it because you're foreign." An advantage, I think, to a writer, this ability to shut out trivialities.

❀ 🌀🌀🌀 ❀

The End of the Affair

Just like the beginning,
Eddying over the rough spots,
Glistening in still backwaters,
It imperceptibly edges
Into the acceptable
—Not so different from wading into cold waves,
Thinking you aren't able,
Groping assurances of smooth shale.
You shrug shoulders,

Hug arms to chest,
Gird up your loins...resist
Till the riptide in your blood surges
And suddenly you're swimming
As another sort of creature,
The scent of the sea
Familiar as the body of your lost love.

Winter Morning

Not a new idea—I saw a painting just the other day:
A woman of huge round eyes and large bosom,
Her mantle a sea of white sailboats and dolphins.
So on a chill winter morning
When I want to burrow deeper
Into the warm caves my body has dug in the bedding,
I think of the silk kimono
I will wear,
Embroidered with clashing dragons,
Flying golden fish, the rising sun,
Silver cuttlefish and seaweed and shells.
My flesh will burn with cold
And a fire roar in the furnace
Under my skin.

MICHAEL WATERS

I first visited Greece in 1971, heading for Mykonos, but realized as the ship entered the harbor that every other backpacker on board had that same destination. I asked a crewman where the boat docked next. "Ios," he replied, and kissed his fingertips. From that port I climbed the road into town, then stumbled down the goat path to Milapotas where I spent the next three weeks. There was one small *taverna* at each end of the crescent beach, few people, and a gorgeous villa set in the center of the half-moon. Each day I peered through its blue gates and wondered who was lucky enough to live there. A decade later in 1982, having taught for a year at the University of Athens, I found myself on the hill just behind it, renting the stone cottage that belonged to its owner, an  American woman who'd built the villa in 1966. I lived and wrote in that cottage with its view of the sea off and on during the following decade.

I don't know what drew me to the Greek islands in 1971—probably Henry Miller's *The Colossus of Maroussi*—or why I left three weeks later. I was twenty-one, and there were other countries to visit. But even early on, Ios seemed a spiritual home of sorts, one place where the modern world didn't intrude. After I drew water from the well in the morning, I had nothing to do all day but walk the island, swim, and write. Isn't that one version of the writer's life that sparks the adolescent imagination? I found that such a life could be true. A stone cottage lit by kerosene lamp under constellations reflected in the Aegean—except for my battery-operated cassette player, I could have been living in a previous century.

Greece helped me realize the value of a life stripped of most distractions. I still struggle these days to see beyond my walls of books and the boundaries of academic life, but Ios—a state of mind now if not the island itself—sustains me. The daily text of earth and wind and sun and sea—that elemental alphabet—still seems endlessly readable in the light that beckons me back as it draws me forward.

Parthenopi

Ios

Once we beheld the brilliance of our estate
reflected in the haloed serenity of the girl
who prepared the basketful of cucumbers for salad,
slicing each nub into watery wheels,
columns of coins in the egg-white bowl.
Then she'd lift each miniature transparency
as she'd seen the priest flourish the Host,
thumb the serrated blade
to nick the green, then twist her wrist
to peel back the dust-plumed skin, the rubbery shavings
heaping a wild garden, unspoiled Eden, on the wooden counter.
Again and again she consecrated each wafer.
We basked in her patience, that rapt transportation,
her bell-shaped, narrowing eyelids as she spun
one papery sun, then the next, her perfect happiness,
smoke from the blackened grillwork wreathing her hair,
the fat of the slaughtered lamb hissing in the fire.
Her name—we'd asked our waiter—was Parthenopi, "little virgin."
We were still a couple then, our summer's lazy
task to gather anecdotes toward one future,
each shared and touching particular
to be recited over baked brie and chilled chardonnay
in the grasp of some furious, if distant, winter.
"Parthenopi," one of us might say, chiming a glass,
but the common measure of love is loss.
The cucumbers glistened in oil and thyme.

Scorpions

How easy, lazy in this light-struck country,
    to grow familiar with the morning
        rituals: boil water from the well,

hang the empty egg basket on a nail
    for the frail farmer to fill,
        prop open shutters with rocks.

And rocks are more than abundant here
   where a man must shake his shoes
      like a nervous gambler at The Sands,

say, rattling his fist, then
   staring at what spills out—
      constellations of scorpions,

Rorschach blots come alive, the color
   of rancid butter, that yellow-going-to-brown,
      miniature skeletons awaiting flesh.

They click, broken dice, onto the stone
   floor, then scuttle into cracks
      before I bring the heel down.

Once I was stung on the thumb
   by a thimble-sized scorpion,
      and twice I've found two

locked together at the pincers,
   performing some arachnid mating
      magic or macabre toe-to-toe tango.

If you breathe on a scorpion,
   legend tells us, it burns bright blue,
      but whose lips would draw so close?

Yet who could consign even one
   to the lower concentrics of hell
      without regard to grand design?

Consider their power: to make a man
   meditate, ignore the sun
      to gaze into the shadows in his shoes.

Ios
1987

Two Baths

One

Lovelier than Susannah
who set the elders' hearts groaning at twice their faithful
stride, so that each grandfather
clutched his breast to remember the beauty of the nude
female body, you tilted
the pail to plash well water over stepped terraces
of flame-red hair, rivulets
snaking down breasts, God-thumbed birth-stain, vulval thatch and thighs.
And I lavished the shampoo
as you knelt in the rue anemone, spiraea's
windfall stippling burnished skin,
lather foaming through my fingers, foaming shut your eyes
as you took me in your mouth,
the sun bearing witness to our blind, intuitive
coupling, till I tipped the pail
to rinse our fallen flesh, let our imperfections glisten.

Two

Light roused us from the depths of our separate longings
and while I balanced buckets
you laced black sneakers for your morning run on the cliff,
wrapped the red ribbon of shirt
around your forehead, stretched stiff calf muscles, then ran off.
I could see you jog the beach
as I arranged notebooks, pens, on the marble table,
then begin the zigzagging
goat path toward the crag overlooking our stone cottage,
your red rag still visible
against the rough, anaemic marble of the mountain.
Remember the undressing,
how I slipped off your Nikes, peeled each slick of cotton,
then unknotted the sweatband
and dipped that tatter into the icy water, sponge
pressed between your breasts, your legs,
the tenderness between us before the sex turned sour?—

before your six miles became
a more-than-tacit withdrawal, like sleep, or headphoned jazz,
so I'd watch you crest the hill
as I worked at the marble table, wrenching lines, syllables, the diminishing
sweatband a raw wound in the distance, as I revised
draft after draft, prodding you
past the horizon, writing you out of existence.

Well Water

The slender wire of the handle
insists itself in the fist,
the tin pail clatters
its history of consonance,

and the knotted rope
snakes round the pulsing wrist.
Naked, sleep-lulled, ambiguous,
I follow the twisting, narrow

path clumped with thistle,
clamber the loosening wall
to the cool, secluded
circumference of the well.

I release the pail upside-down
to break the stippled skin,
to allow the wakening water
slowly to seep in,

then haul, knot by knot,
the brimming pail over the rim.
Off balance, splotching the trail,
I heft home the tin pail

solid with the clarity of water,
its sweeping, blue parcel of sky
a metaphor of the mind
rehearsing its startled fluency.

Each morning I begin again,
drinking from the pail my fill
of the brassy, generative water,
the raised, resourceful syllable.

Ios
1985

Akrotiri

"Is it because there is no word
tender enough to be your name?"
—James Joyce, "The Dead"

We visit the house where the famous mural
depicting two boys boxing was found,

and a cache of clay jars
glazed with blue octopi,

a bathtub, a hairbrush—
these last remnants of civilization

stored millennia ago
by strata of volcanic ash that fell

only to be brushed away
and carted, now, to the thrashing sea.

The lost skyline, the olive window-frames,
the beauty buried below the cinders

are swept again by salt and light—
the kindled terraces are bare,

the avenues narrow enough
to hold you near me

as I touch your hair
and breathe your ancient name in Akrotiri.

Thira
1985

Black Olives

In those days while my then-wife
taught English to a mustached young nurse who hoped to join
her uncle's practice in Queens,
I'd sip gin on our balcony and listen to her
read aloud from the phrasebook,
then hear the student mimic, slowly, *Where does it hurt?*
then my wife repeat those words
so the woman might enunciate each syllable,
until I could no longer
bear it, so I'd prowl the Ambelokipi district
attempting to decipher
titles emblazoned on marquees—*My Life As A Dog,*
Runaway Train, Raging Bull—
then stroll past dark shops that still sold only one item—
kerosene, soap, cheese, notebooks—
to step down into the shop that sold olives, only
olives in barrels riddling
a labyrinth of dank aisles and buttressing brick walls.
I'd sidle among squat drums,
fingering the fruit, thumbing their inky shine, their rucked
skins like blistered fingertips,
their plump flesh, the rough salts needling them, judging their cowled
heft, biding my time. Always
I'd select a half-kilo of the most misshapen,
wrinkled and blackest olives
sprung from the sacred rubble below Mt. Athos, then
had to shout "Fuck Kissinger!"
three times before the proprietor would allow me
to make my purchase, then step
back out into the smut-stirred Athens night to begin
the slow stroll home, bearing now
my little sack of woe, oil seeping through brown paper,
each olive brought toward my mouth
mirroring lights flung from marquees and speeding taxis,
each olive burning its coal-
flame of bitterness and history into my tongue.

JOSEPH STROUD

I came to Greece in the spring of 1975. Greece was the last stop on a voyage around the world that began in the South Pacific and gradually moved west, passing through Australia, Southeast Asia, India, and on through Pakistan, Afghanistan, Iran, and Turkey. By the time I arrived in Greece I had been on the road for almost a year, and I was looking for a place that was remote, quiet, and uncrowded, where I could stop and let my spirit settle. I found that place in the village of Olimbos on the island of Kárpathos in the Dodecanese. Olimbos was a village the modern world had passed over. It was situated on the saddle of a mountain, the Aegean on one side, a rocky valley on the other. It had no electricity; there were no vehicles, no hotel, no restaurant, one small *taverna*. The people spoke a Doric-inflected Greek; grew their food in terraced plots on the mountainsides; kept chickens, pigs, donkeys, and goats; handloomed their own clothes; and made music with lute, lyre, and goatskin bagpipe. I rented a room above a house and stayed there for five months.

I soon settled into a simple rhythm—mornings I worked through my notebooks and journals, trying to make poems, and afternoons I walked in the mountains around the village. It was a severe landscape—sky, sea, rock—washed clean by the Aegean light. To hold a poem up to that light was to see the poem's structure and flaws, to see through the posturing and gimmicks, the slickness that so much writing is made of. It's been thirty years since my stay in Olimbos. I have never gone back. But to this day every poem I write I hold up to the memory of that landscape and the clarity of that light.

Our Blood Is Red Coral,
We Build a Bridge Over the Abyss

I don't know if Kazantzakis ever walked the mountains of Kárpathos.
Or visited the village of Ólimbos that looks down on the Aegean.
Above the pines are the orchards of stone and light. No one lives there.
But one day while walking I heard a music—bagpipe and small bells
followed by a shepherd with his goats—up there, in midsummer,
in the furnace of the sun, in that place even the gods have abandoned.

Crossing the Island

(Kárpathos, twenty years ago)

Heat heat and the sky a flame of sapphire
an ocean of fire even rocks blazing
the earth a rush of coals Aegean summer
the air still the day dead center in the sun
the world without breath even the goats
drinking light all morning have descended
to the shade of a cistern while out there
the blue of the ocean and the other blue of sky
come together in that place where the gods
descend to this world and enter
the heavy honey of the body and it was on
this day when I set out into the core of light
wondering what it would bring for I knew
for once and for good my marriage was over
and henceforth there would be only these excursions
into the sun into the body and the world
would exact its praise of basil or goats or the smell
of thyme and the resin and gold pitch of pine
and all the shelters of the spirit began crumbling
within me as I dismantled the man I was
learning to replace the old belief of Latin
with the new tongue of this world the tongue
of rock and mountain and memory of the woman
washing her hair on the terrace in the granite light
as I went through the day to the other
end of the island where the wedding guests
had butchered a goat and roasted the meat

over a fire in a noon so bright I couldn't see
the flames as if sunlight were searing the flesh
and the bride looked upon it all and found it
to her liking as the groom carved the meat
passed it around and we ate of the world
and so it would continue.

NICHOLAS SAMARAS

Living abroad is a coloring, a way of self-discovery and self-evolving—a process akin to an earthen mirror. As a writer I deal with what affects me, what I experience, and writing is my way of expression, of making sense of things. Every writer cannot, must not, stop growing. And anything foreign and new is an impetus, a catalyst. Therefore, I needed Europe, the strangeness of it. I lived abroad, simply, to become changed.

Emily Cantrell

As we are writers, the enemy is subjectivity; the saving influence is objectivity, what we strive for in order to see things clearly and to express them artistically. My goal is to express my world and experience as originally as possible. Being American is a thought process. And only another country can show you this. It is the way you walk, the way you gesture, the manner in which you eat, the clothes you wear. Even the way you stand when listening to someone or waiting at an intersection broadcasts your nationality. Living abroad is an interaction and separation, and the combination of the two suddenly seen as if at a distance is a revelation and growth to cherish. I felt like a witness to my own life as my American priorities shifted and changed, the sphere of myself expanding.

All of this is how my living in Greece changed and influenced me. I realized the greatest cure for writer's block is an airline ticket, the slapping reality of seeing outside of oneself. In Europe, for the foreigner there is no stagnation or complacency; there is only today, the now. Along the way and through the years, what I have with me are the record and witness, the writings I produced and the person I am continually becoming.

Amphilohios

This is the first thing you think of.
It may be the way he fills the room,
how morning light seems to flow over him
and is absorbed into his black cassock.
Immediately, this man, his
long, thick salt-and-pepper beard,
will cause you to think of little else,
will have you realise your future
is never yours
but a wind you may
only tack against.

Because you have never felt anything as
love without possession,
you could think he will want
something, eventually.
You think of everyone
who has ever wanted of you,
think of yourself
who has wanted of your life the most.
But he is simple in greeting,
muslin arms outstretched, shaking
the light from his body.

For three days, he will love you and ignore you—
something you find both appreciated and disappointing.
It is strange how you almost miss the judgment.
Into evening, he sits at a carved
table and studies; you sit
opposite, writing cards or gazing past the balcony,
learning how not to start a conversation.
Looking out to a blue vestment of sky,
you think a benign love is possible.
The weekend visit becomes an icon
burning into your sleep.

Before you are ready to give
this up, through a blue-veined wind,
the long boat at midnight leads
its ghostly wake into the harbor,

its fogbell calling.
At the wharf, you look out over the black-robed water.
Father holds you in the lightest way
goodbye, kisses your cheeks, his neutral
beard brushing you like air.
And you love the way you are
lost in the openness of his face. You love
the way you are lost.

Crossing the Strait

Behind me, Ouranopolis softens in the distance.
The channel crinkles in the supply-boat's wake
and it is too late to return to what I know.
Ahead lies the Athos peninsula, a blur of monasteries.
The boat creaks on the water, under my bootsoles.
Waves slap against the prow.
The backwash fans out, melts into itself.

On the late cusp of winter, there is
a sound to blackness!
Hoarse wind chuffs into my dufflecoat
as white-caps churn.
The boat falls on choppy swells, knocks me
back into wooden crates and hemp-twine.
Gulls wheel leeward, the wind unstrings them.
The few oil-grey dolphins that teased the bow
submerge with deft fluke strokes.
Slapping each wet hurdle, spray spatters me.
I lick the salt from my knuckles.

Athos approaches, mute, expectant.
The sealine serrates the beach.
I hesitate to go further, to face
the noise within me
in such silence.
What will my own voice sound like?
The boat smacks the quay
and the captain cleats the line
to a stump of flaking iron and concrete.

Leagues above, the monastery juts from the cliff.
Two monks perch on the wooden overhang, grasp the railing.
The dark gaps of broken planks below their feet.
Their charcoal robes billow and clutch
their tenuous bodies.
They call down, their voices drown.
Their mouths are lost
in massive, darkly-flowing beards,
little mouthing O's.
In contrast, their fingers are spokes of white light.
The monks gesture, wave quickly into their chests.
Grigora, Apano!
But I can't climb and the steps from the sea
are wet, heavy with moss.

The Distant, Watery Globe

This is the grey smudge of time.

Precarious ascent. A place light-
refracted and shimmering.
The far away close to touch.

I rest on a fragile balcony
edging
the space of the world.

Between my scuffed shoes
and the greywood boards,
the sheer cliff dives below.

Vision tenses and swims
when high winds groan louder,
straining the parapet's shaky wood.

Through the hours of no horizon,
nothing but the outlying, hazed
blue of water fading

into the hazy beginning of atmosphere.
No difference where

water ends and sky.

In this rarity of air,
I put up my hand to pluck the floating sky,
palm away a cup of blue.

Down and away, distance
flees from us.
Half-visible, the red liquid

of the sun's corona
drowns last distinctions,
enters us into a world

of lamp shadow and slicklight.
I could be happy apart from my life
where these hours and curvatures bring me.

For days, I surface
into a thin spirit
of morning air to view

wispy-tissued clouds veiling
the hillsides, yellow sun pooling
shards of mirrors on the ocean.

Everything smoky and quiet.
The breath and scent of green leaves.
The trilling of birdlife.

Haven't you ever wanted to be so immersed?
I would live here on Oros, finally
alone with silence

and wavering light,
in a simple hut,
a fireplace

and wood for winter,
a spot on the floor for a bed,
the fluency of prayer everywhere.

Give me the space to go grey with this,
the watery height and rim of the globe,
the one distance

further than time.

Lovely for the Sharing,
Lonely among the Beautiful

Where the smooth cobbled alleys become aimless, I walk.
Where the colored brochure calls exotic, romantic, I walk

without someone's ear to hear me, another's eye to apprehend
with me all this, all of this. The Arabian flavor, the Orthodox

foundations, the warmth of history in these walls, the minarets,
domes, and ancient songs. My God, the waft of spices in the air.

Yet elsewhere. Someone is elsewhere. My shadow elongates
ahead and darkens the stones, deepening the echo of footfalls,

double footfalls. How distraction can focus back. What is beauty
when there's no one beside you, a loved one to nudge and say,

"Look. Look at this. It's lovely"? Oh, lovely for the sharing.
Without that, what are these streets of light and easy play

I stroll without purpose or direction? How light
is exotic air with the weight of absence on me?

Wavering in a guided land, where anything
truly beautiful is only loneliness for another—

without someone beside me to share this with,
everything lovely is exactly half, and I am

lonely among the beautiful.

ALICE FRIMAN

It is difficult to talk about the influence of Greece on my poetry; more to the point is the influence of Greece on my life. In 1977 at the age of forty-two, I took off for Athens. I had no hotel reservations and no itinerary. I just went. Later I would say that if I had known what I would find there, I'd have *stolen* the money to go. I went to find the roots of all the things I loved—drama, history, philosophy, poetry. I went to find the old gods, if you will. I went as a personal odyssey—the voyage out a mirror image of the voyage in—staying away from other tourists. I found a country of incomparable beauty and wildness. The next summer I returned. I felt as if I had come home.

Ron Price

Stumbling on Paradise

How much were the stars that night
Down like lanterns green-swinging.
The moon creaming the water
Dancing naked in all that shining.
In Kyparissia the sun sets into the
Middle of the sky before it hits the sea,
Tucks like a nickel in a slot
And everyone goes up the hill to
Sip ouzo and watch it drop.
In Kyparissia the apricot tree
Mingles with spearmint and bursts
Golden in the glare of the Greek
Sun streaming off Alekos in the
Red truck going for roast lamb and

Wine and Bread. Lighting his cigarette,
Drinking the smoke like a thirst.
And only in Kyparissia tastes
Like that, smells like that
With the sand white and the
Stars rising over his shoulder
And me wrapped to him and
Saying his name, saying his name
Beyond wondering why or how
All the lines could come together like that
Like the arrows in a tulip's throat
Or the needles in a rose quartz eye.

Stars

Heraclitus said
stars are bowls of inverted fire.
In Delos, yes, where they hang from ropes
or Kyparissia, holding up the soft-backed black
like buttons in a love seat. Here
the world's infection makes them dim.

I remember a Greek night,
counting the spread of stars above my head
plus the two broken in his eyes—
a Peloponnesian beach and me
clinging to him, *Alekos,* saying
Alekos, until the moon rose
bleaching the sky tame. Even I
turned alabaster. While behind him, the waves
bunched and groaned under their fallen cargo—
the gleaming crockery of the drowned.

Now, the sky is filled with ghosts:
ashes in the bottom of their bowls
too deep even for the winds
that prowl down the skies sniffing at rims,
howling for a wildness that burns.

WILLIAM PITT ROOT

In 1971 I took the ferry to Hydra, and a woman on it said, "The poet just left the island," and I said, "What poet?" expecting to hear an exotic unfamiliar name. She said, "Why, Leonard, Leonard Cohen." I knew his first couple of LPs, *Spicebox of Earth,* an early Canadian Film Board flick on his poetry (in which he shows his unmistakable talents as a standup comic), but I hadn't known he was in Greece on this then-paradaisical island. I swam as often as I ate, mingling with the foreign tourists, walking under the sun, under the moon and stars, sleeping half my nights outside in sparse grass near cliffs above the sea. One day a huge German sailboat anchored in the harbor, and all night it broadcast recorded speeches of Hitler as its clearly fabulously wealthy owner and company cavorted conspicuously throughout the village. I was astonished that no Greek killed them. And also disappointed. I saw an Eden projected by my ignorance suddenly overshadowed by this rude reminder of its history.

Pamela Uschuk

In 1984 I traveled to Samos with my wife to meet Yannis Ritsos. We spent an evening talking about poetry—he showed us three manuscripts written in his impeccable hand and said the few changes meticulously penned in the margins were the only revisions he had done. From his years as a political prisoner, he showed us dozens of the hundreds of stones with the faces he had drawn on them to bemuse and disarm the suspicions of guards. He would gift his keepers with those faces in exchange for more ink, pens, and nibs. He hid enough poems to fill several volumes each time he was released. I asked if he had any advice to help aspiring poets, such as taking creative writing classes in the United States. He narrowed his eyes and smiled at the notion of such poets, such classes, then said, "There's no way to help a poet, [long pause] and there is no way to hurt a poet, either, if the poet is a poet." His, of course, was just the authority that could utter such a thing without false modesty or vanity. There was not a trace of bitterness apparent in him either. That whole evening he was high-spirited and passionate. As we left, one of our friends who had translated his remarks for us shyly told him he had once, decades before, written a poem for her mother on one of the islands where he had been held. "Her name?" Then he nodded, looking closely at our friend, Elena. "I remember your mother, but do you remember that I also wrote a poem for you?" Then he recited it to her from heart. As he spoke tears filled her eyes. When he finished he held her, a 30-year-old woman, as if she were still four or five. I was struck quite dumb both by his memory and by the unmistakable dimensions of his heart. From his modest home we went to the nearby moonlit sea and took turns sitting in the concrete throne the people of the village had made for Ritsos to sit in while he watched the endless succession of his beloved waves.

The influence of such moments, and countless others, was diffuse rather than specific. One of the most striking impressions certainly was the recognition of how widely known and deeply respected Greek poets are in their homeland, by cobblers and ships' crews, by taxi drivers and clerks. Even a poet as complex as Ritsos, is as integral to the culture as rock stars are in the United States. It is a stimulating corrective to the odd lot that falls to most American poets at home.

With No Other Witness

for Yannis Ritsos

In Greece I met a man who wrote for years in exile on an island,
wrote with no other witness than sea-wind and the ranked blue waves,
wrote on scraps of thin paper skinned from precious cigarettes
stitching poems rolled-up like toothpicks into his trouser-cuffs,
permitting guards to believe that his pen was treasured
for stones, for finding faces in the stones
    and drawing them out, feature by feature,
some as gifts for the villagers, others for the guards themselves
    to give their sweethearts.
Dispensing those cigarettes he hoarded so carefully,
watching him sit all those years among stones
    washed up by his beloved sea
and bent inexhaustibly to his task,
Harmless enough, they may have thought,
with all the Aegean for an audience!

All the world's more like it.
                Decades later, free,
still within hearing of the unimprisonable waves,
he gestures to pine shelves lining his study,
pointing with his cigarette. "I could put faces on those stones

to bribe guards and please strangers—take one
for yourself, and here, have this one for your wife—
but my true passions were unmasked in poems
read today in forty-seven tongues." Nor, he adds,
smiling, have those sweethearts in the villages
quite yet forgotten him.
                    Guards, beware of charmers
when even the nations of stones return their gaze.

Orpheus Reconsidered

It had been some time, as you'll remember,
since he'd seen her.

And time which, for the living, flashes
for the dead drags.

Down there among the joyless shades
he took no food, but she

being educated in an epic hunger
and knowledge of the bone

had long since grown quite ravenous,
her sweet eyes savage flames

and her heart a cauldron
of scoured emptiness

in which his richest wildest lyrics
rang too thin, too tame

so when he'd struck the bargain
we all know, and turned

to start the long climb back
still piping his tune,

before they'd gone halfway
she filled with scorn

since he would not regard her
there behind him

seething with resentments
no simple lyric could appease:

If he could not love

her cheeks of ash,
her lips of carrion,

her heart half-wed now
to an elder darkness,

she would not belong to a boy
who kept his word to demons

rather than to his own heart.
She turned before he turned

to find her gone. And she fed
on the promises Death kept.

ELENI SIKELIANOS

The first time I traveled to Greece I was nineteen, and I felt an incredible sense of freedom and joy. It was there that I allowed myself to commit my life to writing. I went to Greece because of a family connection. I keep going back because I love the landscape, the sea, the history, the literature, the light, the food, and (much of the time) the people. I leave each time because Greece is not my permanent home. There are many ways in which the culture is not mine, and I am sometimes uncomfortable in the balkanized view of geography and ethnicity, and in the narrow strictures that a national religion can impose. Nevertheless, I am more comfortable there in ways I might not be in the States—there is a kind of freedom of which the Greeks are very proud. Greece is not my home, but it is another home for me.

Lisa Jarnot

Thus, it has added another landscape, another layer of language, a whole battery of histories and literature to my resources as a writer. Even when I am not in Greece my work continues to be informed by the place. Of course, the history of Greek thought and poetry and art is strong, and all these elements become embedded in my ideas of the landscape, which in turn have become part of my person (in the way that everything I have ever read or seen or done does). This information, intellectual and visual and spiritual, is waiting in recesses to be drawn upon when necessary, wherever I am.

Shadows of a Gazetteer

What is this city in which we sit here?

The smooth plausible green
Ruins of this town or that

To inquire of the stones & fields & compile: What are your thoughts
    on history, what happens
        after death?

After death, you will feel gravity in each tiny muscle
        of the face move more precisely, hear

      Neanderthals playing through bone-pipes

      powder blasts of snow, ice like a lead glove thieving
      over trees

      You will arise, go to Ninevah
      (she goes West instead, to Tarshish)

      If you find anything, you will find everything, thus it follows
      you will find everyone

      not the dream with the devils in it
      not the dark Armageddon

      but the dream of the ancient walled city in the sloping dark
      a red paper garland strung about the place to look
          like poppies fluttering in the breeze—

      the most delicate constructions, like bubbles—They are poems. Know
      the most deliciousest honeyishness;

      the black stars over Lakonia;
      the quick liquefaction of cats in the night; life,

      life in its accessories & motives; music
      & gymnastics that render it smoothish. Before death

mind lies in the lap
of the dabbling heart, it is a doubling

of heat
touching life at a tangent

Man lies in the lap, woman, of an immense volcanic harbor tonight.

First Greek Poem

I the roses love in the garden of Adonis
I the salted fry of marguerite love, the one chamomile, the tiny white that snaps
    dancing in the gutter with funny
I reddest poppy painted in blood love
Love I the final columned crown
Ever a flower inventory wept, I dreamt
Of death, wedding flower; treading
purple will I go
Into that drowning house
With wet little lambs one-day old *(arnakia),* white horses *(waves)* lapping
    at the heart-knobs
When the slave pumped the handle, and the water rose

> *(the first known organ is a Greek water organ; slaves*
> *were required to pump the handle to make the water rise)*

Footnote to the Lambs

1. You shall hope to know the power of the imagination
2. You shall wish to be intellectual, be somebody; you shall
    forget about bombs
3. You shall dream of a caravan circling lush trees
    & live in dirt balls, with no sugar, no swaying allowed
4. You, loveliness in your Grecian tires, good citizens
    of sheepdom, smoking hashish, hush
5. You shall come from the Azure

Histories: The Pots & Pans of Early Greece

The pots & pans
of early
Greece were really
breakable, red-
figured, black, silhouettes banging
around Herakles'
knees; but even He
was "more than a woman," circa 1973
in the spirit of '76 to get
out, busting moves on the well-lit dance floor, who learned his letters
from the fertile crescent, to call Anaximander's "something"
energy. We were...of all that happened
in the *petite patrie* of Sophokles—boys under the sheets
with their mothers. Parmenides
suggested where to hook faith in the mouth, that substance
of things looked for
but not received, hectic & reeling
into the centuries' sleep. Heraclitus

looked at the same world and came
to other conclusions, like Strife, when the
never-ending fire seems to strike
the strobe light dead, twice. This is the story of our reckless
lineage, the beginning of the road we trod in the
brotherhood of beings of primeval days, a
collapsible House of Origins appearing from its palace-
prison, a human ghost loved in the shape of a swan
under the heights

Film: How to Exploit an Egg

from the material body or the material
that makes up a body (textiles, dry goods)
or the materials from an

egg including nitrogen &
I want to make a green

film in which
Clytemnestra comes back
& an egg is divided
into sun, & a moon
which spreads
over the sky like

whites and in the
patates of patates in the
myth of the rape
of potatoes I would put

a woman
back in the sky, a woman
dancing in a mask made by Eleni
on a screen of grey which is a blue

film of the myth
of all Sisyphus. She is dancing on the small
cubits
of microspace
which make up the rocks

—Wherefore speak you so, Stranger?

—Is it me you mean?

—It is you I mean, I mean you, Stranger
  voice voicing the material body in shiny anterooms

Moon, O moon, hearken
& reflect: this egg-house made to birth surfaces liquid & curved

Said egg, come, mock rock & bone
come, skull, shell, hull formed inside
come, ship, brains, & beans
o, come, paw, dabble & dangle in sugar pools
Said curved egg, come, claw
come, cigars sent by lords
come, liver, come fur, be birthed
& bent space itself will truly think in every limb & velocity of stars

Essay: Delicately

The father pollutes his body and
this is illegal and yet he does not
knowingly or purposefully pollute rivers
except by the small necessities
of daily living. Chevron pollutes rivers
and dirt and children are born
into brain cells in wrong places. If my father
smokes in a public place, this could
get him into trouble. If he shoots
heroin at home and someone
official finds him he
will be fined or arrested, maybe jailed.
This is the classic story in which a hero
sets out on a voyage, like Homer's or Dante's, and
along the way finds out something about
her/himself, only this time there's nothing
left to find out. For the world like Sappho was either

small, dark, and ugly
or small, dark, and beautiful.

David Mason

I went to Greece almost by accident in 1980 with my first wife. By sheer luck we ended up renting the house of an American professor in Mani.

After eight months there we had five more delicious months in a one-room hut in a little bay called Kalamitsi where our closest neighbors were Joan and Paddy Leigh Fermor. They have been deeply important friends to me ever since. But my time in Kardamyli also was the beginning of other formative friendships and my first experience of learning a language through total immersion. Though I never have had the luxury of studying Greek in a  classroom and often feel the inadequacy of my language abilities, what Greek I possess remains one of my abiding pleasures. The language is for me a complex feast of historical and aural associations, sophistication, ribaldry—poetry itself, really.

After that first stay in Greece we returned to the States so I could work for a film company, and in the next few years my life was pretty well torn to shreds. The marriage ended, I drifted from job and job, and though I attempted to keep up my Greek I felt as if the whole Greek experience was lost to me. Luckily, I met Yiorgos Chouliaras, then press attaché in New York City, and we began a long collaboration on translations of his poems, which have since appeared in magazines all over the world. Through Yiorgos I met many other Greeks and Greek-Americans, improved my Greek by increments and maintained some sense of a connection with the country. It was a long haul getting my life back on track, but Greece remained a touchstone experience for me, a source of hope and pleasure. Finally in 1996 I was able to get back to the country for a few weeks, then in 1997 I had the luxury of spending half a year there on a Fulbright artist-in-residence fellowship. My landlady for several months was Katerina Anghelaki-Rooke, who at once became one of the great friends of my life. I was able to reconnect with old friends in Kardamyli and elsewhere and to meet new friends among Greeks and Grecophiles. Katerina, appalled by my grammar, set me to work improving my Greek yet again. Unfortunately, my increasing hearing loss makes my absorption of language more and more difficult with time, but I still work at it.

In 2001–02 I was able to return to Greece again, this time adding visits to Turkey, which have deepened my appreciation of the region. I have fast friends in several Aegean locales now, the cities as well as the villages, and they remain a huge part of my waking and dreaming life. At one time Greece was a rather romantic place for me since I didn't really have to work there—it appealed to the adolescent in me. Now I feel more capable of loving her in all her complexity, if you'll forgive my use of the gendered allusion. I know that I will never know her as deeply as I would like. She has given me gifts I can never fully repay: language-love, friendship, impulsive moments, conversations, memories—all of which I am trying to make sense of in a volume of memoirs I'm currently writing.

Schoolchildren at Mistras

Snow falls above the smoky vale of Sparta
in mountains where the weak were once abandoned.
Everywhere you turn, the old world is unearthed
between the shops where citizens still wait
for a change of season, or, outside of town,
gather the olives, crate the winter oranges.

A hush ascends the ruined holy city
from the stare of Christ to battlements above,
from the nun who leads her three goats out to grass
and almond trees that blossom another snow—
silence these schoolchildren happily shatter,
as if escaping death in the museum.

Acrostic from Aegina

Anemones you brought back from the path
Nod in a glass beside our rumpled bed.
Now you are far away. In the aftermath
Even these flowers arouse my sleepy head.

Love, when I think of the ready look in your eyes,
Erotas that would make these stone walls blush
Nerves me to write away the morning's hush.
Nadir of longing, and the red anemones
Over the lucent rim—my poor designs,
X-rated praise I've hidden between these lines.

Pelicans and Greeks

Edward Lear in San Remo, Italy, 1888

Nights when he cannot sleep, Lear looks for paper,
uncertain whether he should sketch or write,
or which of his living friends might comprehend
his travels off the rough and tumble roads

As soon as I picked up my pen I felt
I was dying.

           And should he then have married?
On such long nights, lines from the Laureate
chase through his brain like notes flung off the scale—
and infant *with no language but a cry....*

What of Bassae, the temple on the mountain,
the ancient oaks still stretching out their arms
to sunlight he had tried to catch in oils?
Who owned that painting now? How could one own
the love that lay behind it? All the years
and all the travels must mean a little more
than light that dies along the temple flutings.

Laden with lunch, the drawing boards and paints,
Georgis played Sancho Panza to his knight.
Dear Georgis—you who witnessed wonders with me....
Spoken to nothing but an empty room.

On Crete a black man came, and little boy,
and peasants, and I drew them. They were all
good tempered, laughing. I remember how
the small boy saw my drawing of a donkey

and almost cried and was impelled to give me
lemons as a gift. I gave him a pencil.
A gesture I can't forget, ingenuous
and awkward like the play of pelicans—
the ordinary beauty of the world
that makes one jubilate in sheer delight
and shudder when we feel life leaving us.

In India an English schoolgirl came
to meet the painter, having memorized
"The Owl and the Pussycat." Such was fame.
And there was Georgis who was mad again
because he could not ride an elephant.
And there were mountains higher than the ones
he loved in Crete and Thessaly. They too
compelled the draughtsman's longing not to lose
minute sensations he had drawn upon,
fleabags and palaces, pelicans and Greeks.

If no one bought my drawings I should live
on figs in summertime, worms in winter,
with olive trees and onions, a parrot,
yes, and two hedgehogs for companionship,
a painting room with absolute north light....

So many friends are gone. No partner frets
that he cannot sleep, no child arrives to scold him.
He is the sum of all that he has lost,
his hand still dreaming on the empty page.

DON SCHOFIELD

I guess George Seferis brought me to Greece: his poems of exile and loss, his yearning for a place that, when I first visited in the summer of 1976, inexplicably resembled in its topography and its flora and fauna the landscape of my childhood in California's San Joaquin Valley. "Wherever I travel Greece wounds me," he says in one of his poems. I soon understood why, at least in part. Wherever I went during that two-week stay, I found remnants of lost ages, surviving signs of great achievement and terrible catastrophe—not only in the ruins, but even in the names of the warm, generous people I encountered: Penelope, the owner of the pension where I stayed on Syros; Socrates, the man I rented a motor scooter from on Corfu; Ariadne, the flight attendant on my plane to Athens. And I also found, as if shining through cracks in the fallen world, glimpses of a lost Paradise—figs glistening in the gnarled hands of a fruit vendor in smog-choked Ommonia Square; sheep grazing in an empty lot between apartment blocks in suburban Athens; on Syros, through the dust and noise of road construction, a young woman quietly weaving at a big wooden loom on her front porch.

Charles Fishman

Four years later I returned, determined to live and write in Greece as long as possible. In the twenty-three years since, the multiplicities of Greece—urban and rural, historic and modern—have become one of the main subjects in my poetry. The way of life, which so often subordinates order, personal space, quiet, and solitude to emotional expression, intimacy, and personal interaction, is both inspiring and exasperating, challenging me personally and as a writer to let go of certain aspects of my American self and hold more dearly to others. So I still cherish privacy and need a degree of solitude in order to write. But I have learned to let my closest friends come over when they want (without expecting them to call first, as I did in the States) and accept their occasional failure to appear even though we had arranged a rendezvous. Similarly, over the years I have let go of the insular and abstract in my poetry for more direct forms of expression, more concrete imagery, and a more intimate tone. And, just as I am both American and Greek (having recently become a

119

dual citizen), so my poetry often juxtaposes my experience of America, especially the places, people, and events of my California childhood, with the rich reservoir of experience and sensation I have been blessed with during my years in Greece.

Teaching High School in Greece

I wear slacks everyday, teach *Gatsby*
to a class of Yiannakis and Marias, write Emily's
slant truth on the board, check their spelling books
as they carve their desks
with words I can't understand. I tell them

Huck sails the Aegean
on a raft knotted by the
Hero himself. The black stacks of Corinth
remind him of home. Hester loves
the Parthenon, its broken columns with letters
she can touch. Emily circles the Tower of the Winds,
clicking snapshots. Walt hears wind in an Aleppo pine,
thinks North America bigger, greener—endless
next to this thin sighing. Yet he likes it here:
the sunglasses he bought, the postcard
of Diana striding legless.

Truth is, I walk and walk,
not knowing even the alphabet.
Alone at tavernas, I drink retsina late into the night,
but my eyes are wide: This is Greece, I'm here
in the fire of an idea, on a wave of fear and doubt. Figs

brush my cheek when I enter the hotel
where I've learned to keep my dream intact
though the bed in the room above thumps all night
and all morning buses wheeze, trucks
blast past my stop with icons of the Virgin
wired to their grills, motorcycles
race past me on the sidewalk, collect at the light.
From the heart of the traffic I always hear
someone calling: *Helen, Helen.*

Sometimes, when I lean to make a correction,
a young face with ancient eyes
stares back. I'm sure
the dead snake they put in my desk
fell from the Gorgon's head, that I saw
last Sunday, walking through the National Museum,
Emily and Walt holding hands,
leaning close to Persephone,
her smile simple and clear.

The Physics of Parting

A moment ago I heard the fine
spatter of rain in the field behind me,
water rising, ready to sweep me away. Aristotle

taught wet and dry are absolute
opposites, *each on its way*
to its natural place. So why

do I see a row of poplars along a wall
when I turn, wind prying dry leaves
up and down the golden trunks,

and still the hiss of rain in my ears? I think of the spider
weaving that last night it was *our* bedroom,
rising and falling in moonlight,

not like us but Socrates,
who kept standing and sitting those last nights
in his cell, curious about his presence there—

due only to bones and joints
and flexible muscles? the words he uttered
explained just by laws of sound and hearing? I ask

what law for parting lovers,
one wet, one dry? Our wholeness
was never a burden—then it suddenly hardened

in opposite directions. The web snapped in my face
when I finally rose and left, descending
into chaos, but for the mind,

pure and alone, weaving depths
to heights, mind so pure it makes
wings of thick gossamer and lost

love: *rise, now rise.*

Dead Shepherd's Hut

Sure, I can fix the broken door, clear the brush
out front, find a rope and bucket for the well,
a mattress for the iron bed in this hut
I've rented for next to nothing, but what about
his coat and crook still hanging by the mirror,
the photo of bare-breasted women
in white shorts and red boxing gloves
squared-off and whaling at each other?

I've come here, a tangle of desires,
more like the brambles I open the shutters to, the random
twisted olive trees up this valley kilometers from the road,
come to lose myself in the deep lull
of summer, to be less than smoke
curling from a lamp, nothing and nowhere. I like to think

he woke early, herded the huddled goats
up the ridge, that he knew each one by its bell,
that he's still sitting where pine cones
crack in late morning heat, the place
he slipped through to death. He's buried
on the opposite slope, in the one bare patch
among briars and burned grass—*beyond desire,*

I whisper to myself. But when I stand at his rusty basin,
see these women he gazed at every morning,
the smell of leather and sweat implied
by their gleaming shoulders and gloves, the ripple across one breast

where a punch just landed, the spectators cheering
from the darkness surrounding the ring, even the referee
smiling and pointing—I wonder

what he thinks of pleasure now
that he's gone to the source. Dead shepherd,
are you still hovering near your body, or here with me,
gazing at this primal destruction, resenting
even your own birth, that wound that bore you?
Or have you come back with some different knowledge—
taking down your coat and crook
then winking at me with the eyes of a goat, behind their bright slits,
some truth I just can't see.

Callicles Puts a Head on the Argument

...I should not like the argument
wandering about without a head; please then
[Callicles] go on a little longer,
and put a head on.
—*Socrates*

I say pleasure is its own reward.
Nothing to do with order or balance
as the Old Man would have it. It is daring to rise
to whatever might be gathering. Even anger.
That slap from a mistress may bring on
Father, dank with wine and hugs so fierce
they mesmerized. And such music in his voice
as he answered my questions, not like me
bewildered by the bodies of women in the *agora*
pouring out their leeks and winter oranges.

The robber in the alley demanding money—
there's pleasure as he grabs it, and pleasure for the victim
in the stories he'll tell. In the howling of jackals,
the rueful laughter of hyenas,
all we mime in ecstasy.
Such pleasure advancing,
all the prophets cry out
for fiery inundations,

as if anything
could keep us from the sublime.

Give me shadows. Curtains. All morning
in the bath, masturbating to the scent of the woman
last night. Was there temperance in her moans, balance
in the reeds that dangled above us? First I kissed
that perfect crescent, that birthmark on her neck, then sliced it
free. They found her and blame me,
the rabble pounding at my shutters demanding justice.
There's no order to the Cosmos, Socrates,
only the confusion of arms and bellies
rising in the steam around me. I'll dry off

and go out to the mob,
thinking of the pleasure of the pyre that awaits me.
Socrates, I've pressed it in a scroll. I leave it here
for you: That little crescent. That moon
with hair.

Homage to the Wheels

> *Just as if one night
> you happen to enter
> the city that reared you...*
> —George Seferis

Laying down his journal, I think of his life.
        Exile and birth, he spoke of them as one. He escaped
with his parents to this city, where I too fled
        years later, from the opposite direction. In his time
whole empires collapsed, cities razed, his people

driven into the holds of ships, all they managed to save
        grabbed from their hands. My upheavals are nothing
next to his, yet I feel that emptiness he describes,
        that yearning for a past I had to escape. He saw,
when allowed to return as a diplomat, his living room collapsed,

front door now a garden gate, fountain crumbling, graffitied,
        thistles growing in the basin. I saw stacks of books on the porch,

yellowed newspapers, an old woman being wheeled by her daughter
      down the steps, pomegranate gone, pine and eucalyptus.
I too want to know *the mechanism of disaster.*

He went on to become Ambassador to England, won a Nobel. Was it worth it?
      When he died the crowds rioted as they carried his coffin through this
      city
never his, his body their symbol of outrage at the Colonels.
      Exile and birth. In the town where he was born, on bank
and office walls, he saw portraits of the father

of that new country. Downriver from where she was born,
      my mother is dying matter-of-factly. I wonder at my world
where power changes hands with a smoothness he'd envy,
      yet I'm battered like him, broken by oppositions
personal, invisible, in the stretch of body on body, its ramifications.

The dust of events covers what we've lost. Wheels pass over.
      Something new will be ground, I should say, but I won't. This is praise
without hope of renewal, pause in awe of the paths
      we take. I fled my country and wound up not far
from the crossroads where Oedipus killed his father.

Those roads, like the roads of my childhood, are lined
      with eucalypti, olives, cypresses. Here and there
a patch of fur ground into the asphalt.
      The wheels grind.
It just happens.

Adrianne Kalfopoulou

Greece for me is imbued with the ritual of the daily in ways that echo back to childhood: meals that gathered neighbors and relatives, the Easter ritual of painting eggs, exchanging Lambatha candles, dressing up for the midnight mass of the Anastasi. But perhaps more profoundly, the myths and anecdotes of lived historical experiences become a visceral fabric of dailiness in my Greek cultural landscape; history is not so much about formal traditions of classical Greek thought, its mythology and history, as much as it is about the shapes and reverberations of those traditions in their more mundane, anecdotal forms and in the hybrid ways they continue to be expressed within the culture. I am particularly drawn to the emotional power embedded in certain ritualistic contexts, such as the power of Orthodoxy or the Easter celebrations as they are experienced in the secular voices of people. Contemporary Greece is so very disparate and full of mixtures of influence (European, Asian, Balkan) that finally, for me, the ongoing challenge is one of articulating often conflicting, but also exhilarating, multiplicities.

Burgundy

Elina's dress in the run-down house,
deep, wine-colored velvet, the color of Orthodoxy.
Wallpaper in rust-colored edges
and Elina's will to make it beyond this—
another house, the loans all paid, white,
all of it, tiles, walls, floors.

She walks to church, candles bristle in clusters,
faces bloom behind their light.
She prays, she has gone to pray
the future will be otherwise.
Burgundy also, the underwear she wears,
strapless lingerie, the color of
their pain, stockinged along the bed
where the game is dangerous, natural she calls it,
the blood, the desire, the midnight love
in a kitchen of dishes, heaped
in leftovers, uncleaned. Her underwear
and cunt ripped in the struggle
for something more than this life she shares with him—
Taverna nights, the rush of food,
his father aged by the children, later grandchildren,
filling the upper rooms.
There are always the dishes, nights
left with them piled up clean or not
at the same sink edge.

In the dimness is only the color,
black and liquid, the crash, porcelain chips,
Elina's suck of pain hours after the abortion
when he cannot stop, when he takes her,
her white arms, blue eyes, raised in supplication.
She cannot stop the heaving sobs
as he bathes the color away.
He swore later it was love like Claus' *Mavro Daphne,*
the wine named after the dark-haired girl
who drove Claus crazy in so much pleasure.

There is a certain terror in the love
that does not stop with the blood, burgundy
all over the floor, her body,
expensive underwear torn in the taking,
lace and delicate and bought for the moment
prayed after at this other altar
where the priest is missing, and the murmur is a silence
only the initiated understand.

My Daughter's Eyes

My daughter's eyes
have all of Greece, all of Turkey
in their limpid darkness
lightening out of burnt shades of brown.
Wet and jeweled like Asian candy
they will scatter a color so rich
I see Bursa, the *Anatoli,*
deep Aegean velvets that lap the jagged shorelines
of so much discord, so much fevered history.
Her eyes resurrect ancient possibilities, alive
the moment she will insist on truce,
the measured beauty of Platonic balance.
"Why can't you smile at Dad?" she asks,
"why can't you and he be friends?" She is trying
to cross an unknown Bosphorus,
to reach Agia Sofia's gorgeous spires.
But the saints are buried under plaster, their eyes
gouged out—her everlasting *why*
swims the turgid moment. I am her other-
cultured American mother,
her short-tempered efficiency. Her father
is his father's orphaned, barefoot
escape, a Smyrnian memory, the songs she sings
whose words stay foreign and full of intent—
her longing could almost bridge the amber depths,
her eyes ask for the world whole, and I
can only translate so much.

Pergola

1

I see the jasmine blow
the honeysuckle and wild rose stems
which knit the greenest leaves
along green trellis bars.
White butterflies move lazy arcs,
the bees are quiet in the flowers.
In English it is called gazebo,

pergola in Greek. The delicate vines
wrestle, unwind and knot themselves
like strands of hair alive
in a midnight breeze.

2

The one-eyed cat,
the lazy thick-furred grey
has fled the place. Above the tangled vines
the moon casts fragile light
where thistle grows
between the tile, the rotting brittle wood,
a bench once used for tea.

I want to ask Yiayia—
Do the pistachios wave against your mind?
Do you wake to the smell of garden flowers,
Eat jasmine petals and find them sweet?

3

No one waters the vines.
Iron rusts and bleeds a long brown map,
curls down and marks the ground

> *We called it Tsardaki*
> *Little shed in Gypsy*
> *We had grapes too*
> *And Japanese jasmine*

Yiayia spreads spaghetti over cloth,
makes sure the stalks don't break.
Stoops down to lift the leaden pots,
age stealing her strength away.

The loose black slip shows
once her breasts were big, once
we made jam from quince,
squeezed lemons from the garden trees.

One summer long ago
Germans left blood on the kitchen walls

> *Better that I go up like this*
> *My mind, my heart*
> *Have seen too much*
> *All of it black*

4

Now everything's in its place,
the dishtowel rag, oil bottles on tin plates.
She turns to apples boiling on the stove,
makes sure to keep them whole
never uses a fork.

I wipe the marble clean
never leave money where bread is put.

Who stole the yellow carnations?

Her hands rub salt, unfold the towel
to soak up steam.
Her fisted hands pound beef,
clutch all along the counter ledge

> *On Hios the men are gardeners*
> *Women on Andros know to sew*

Her fine-boned ankles
like stems beneath the sagging shift,
her nails all ripped and scratched

> *Each person learns his trade*

5

I move the pans on papered shelves,
the pan she holds tugs muscles
all along her shoulders.

The shift falls down her arm.
She smacks my wrist, spoons
the yellow lengths too quickly
too early in the morning.

Why has the honeysuckle died?
And the food bowl left out for cats
Lies broken in the leaves.

Can't touch this meal she's made for me.

6

The black shift opens at her knees,
she raises lips, her eyes
without the tears, her skin
with sunlight in its lines

> *When you see things*
> *Act like you don't*
> *Like me*

Enough to spread the tablecloth,
make sure the yellow stalks don't break.

Her hands push up as if to cook,
the hands that threaded azure blues
grab slowly at the hanging tubes.

Doctors break skin,
the scarlet spreads and browns
where they push needles in.

7

I know Yiayia, you feel this too,
your body moist, wrists laced
in crimson scars, the cat's deep bites
also around your ankles

Don't smack the cat!
She has your grandfather's soul
That's why she bites

I clean you the way you taught me to,
wipe the breasts he loved,
spoon soup that gurgles in your throat.

The doctors pluck up skin—
find
blue workings
around your wrists and calves

veins break

8

The deadened stems will fly
will bare the bars, skin marked
in rusted shades of red,

hair loosened in a wind of summer vines.
Swinging from the trellis bars, I hear

Ella, ella Adrianoula...

You spoon out sweet vanilla drops

9

Cats stretch and wander in the night

I kiss
the iron cold
lick
where blood has stopped
the hands
so cold
my face against the smell
the mesh of hair
flowering
in this night

I lose you *pergola*
flowering
in these broken strips of rust
I lose you
to the earth
tonight

LONNIE HULL DuPONT

My father was Greek, but I did not know him at all. I met him by accident—I had dropped out of college and taken a job waiting tables in a Greek diner in my hometown.

I looked so much like my father that customers assumed I was one of his children. Consequently, I was able to meet my Greek father. Perhaps this distance from my roots made me more interested in modern Greece. Then I received the opportunity to catapult out of my life for a year and move to the outskirts of Athens to teach English to Greeks.

My Greek experience was largely an urban one, though I saw the countryside and islands on occasion, and I loved every minute of it. I learned to live without a car. I fell in love. I tasted garlic, oregano, lemons. I learned to speak Greek mostly from cabdrivers, who gave me elaborate lessons complete with gestures and who also had the delightful tendency to sing while they drove.

I suddenly had time and permission to write poetry, and it came alive. I was living in a completely different environment for a country girl from Michigan—slowed down, warm, fragrant, a land where people looked into each other's eyes and broke into song for no reason at all. I wrote about my immediate surroundings, my life from a distance, my Greek father.

After a year, I felt the need to come home and face my life again. The Greek sun had baked every drop of Type A personality out of me, and it never returned. I remember on the plane home wanting to stay awake so my year in Greece would not yet be past-tense. I dozed off and jerked awake suddenly with the thought: *How will I live where the men don't sing?*

December on the Ionian Coast

i.

In the train station, coals fall
from the fireplace grate.
Women put down their bags
of garlic and tomatoes
to rub their red hands, to wrap scarves
around themselves. I watch them step out
to those wet and shining streets.

I wait until you come to the door.
You take my hands, hold them
as if you cannot believe I am here.
You press my palms to your dark face.

Outside it is black and rainy, I can hear
the sea. Like children we run
through the quiet village to your house.
Under streetlights you stop to look at me,
laugh out loud at the water in my hair.

ii.

Rain beats its dull sounds, though
I listen for more.
Villagers gather their goats,
their fishing nets. Pigeons shudder
under the eaves. The landlord brings us
bread, rabbit, moussaka.

I try to tell you how it was on the train
when thin sheets of snow spread over the hills;
how everything looked as if there were
one piece of charcoal and a light touch;
how my breath came out of me
in the shape of pears, and watching this
I felt pale and afraid.

You seem only to want
to hear my voice; you say nothing.

Sipping retsina, you follow me,
room to room. I peel oranges in the kitchen,
touch you in the hall, lie with you on the bed.
The shutters ache open this wet night.
We watch our shadows on the wall,
two, then one, and again.

iii.

I walk the mud road into town
followed by chickens, donkeys, and thin dogs.
Old men in bright blue chairs call after me.
They nurse glasses of cloudy ouzo,
their legs crossed at the knee.
Women open windows, spill blankets
to the heavy sky, pin wet linens.
They lean out to watch me,
their breasts resting on their fists.
When I write about this, my left hand
causes a silence in the town. I hear only
the scrape of a chair, the rush of the sea,
those white sheets cracking straight and cold.

Three Marines

In the city of the ancients
the bus rolls through yellow streets.
Athenians clutch the straps and stare
at three Marines fresh from Lebanon, 1983,
their lobotomy haircuts,
bull necks, sneakers.
I know exactly when they will
bend their young knees to squint
through the bright windows: it is near
the gardens, dark and fragrant,
where temples appear like prophets,
older than Christ.
These Marines may not know that,
but surely they sense ruin.
Whatever was familiar, in every port,
floats up and over the pillars of Zeus

to dissolve in arid hills.
Indeed, the Marines lean down,
their tiny cameras bouncing on sunburned arms.
Certainly they will send postcards
to prove they are, in fact, seeing the world.
And the redhead says to me:
Do most of the people here speak American?

LINDA ELKIN

I didn't go to Greece to write. I went to Greece as a dancer. Greece influenced my writing the same way it influenced my life; it gave me the direct

Mark Flower

experience of living close to the sea and the sky. I felt an immediate and lasting resonance with the Greek islands. Although I was a stranger there, I felt I had found one of my true homes.

I spent most of my time outdoors, which was a big change for me as I'd always lived in big cities. I loved to walk on narrow goat trails through the hills, past low stones walls that eventually led to small coves by the sea. I brought very little with me and found I easily could live without my usual habits or distractions. I went to live in a quiet place near the sea—and to stay there long enough so that what was important to me would rise to the surface. Shortly after I returned home, writing became central to my life.

Ancient Game

The women held on to the bull's horns
and jumped, legs suddenly skyward,
swinging their long bodies in a graceful arc
before landing on sure ground.

Over and over they practiced the familiar steps,
trained their sleek bodies to vault
over the earthly weight of the bull,
until their world spun upside down

feet brushing the course of the moon.
For a moment gravity released them:
they rode through the sky
as inviolable as gods.

Clasped hands around curved horns,
they grew accustomed to immaculate timing.
But just when they thought they had mastered
this exacting game of gymnastics, the bull tossed

his wild head and they became women again.
Their bodies in the blue air,
the heat of the brown-haired bull
rising up to meet them.

Amorgos

Just beyond the blue domed church, a marble
woman stands, hidden on an unmarked path.
She no longer has a head, arms or hands.
Even though her face is gone, She watches you.

At first I called her broken, incomplete.
Yet every day as I took my meals and swam
I knew She was standing there above me,
both of us so safe we could have been whole.

The Distance to Katapola

I come from the other side of the island.
It may not seem so far away to you, he said,
as you have taken an airplane and a boat to get here.
But for me it is very far away.

There is a woman who once walked
from where we are standing to the house
I was born in. To walk there could take fourteen,
fifteen, sixteen hours, and you must walk

narrow goat paths on top of the mountains.
The walk to the other side of the island
is very close to the sky, he said.
Can you imagine, to walk from here to there?

It is so far away you might expect another language.
At times I long for my childhood home,
where I lived, as here, very close to the sea.
You have no idea how far it is

as you have taken an airplane and a boat
to arrive where we are standing.
But believe me, I was born in a different
part of the world.

I did not leave the other side of the island
until I was twenty-one, and now to return
is a journey I rarely make, and never in winter
when the seas are rough. I know of a woman

who walked the length of this island.
She walked farther than even the goats have gone.
How can I explain to you how far
I have traveled? If you were to see

the house I was born in, the long path
from the sea leading to that house,
what would you expect? Look at anything here:
this olive tree, that bright red fuschia,

the small yellow cat at your feet. You would see
each of these on the other side of the island
and you would say they are exactly the same.
You would say Dimitri must have forgotten

what it is like to be young. That the trees
must have looked different to him.
Tall trees with the arms of giants.
Dimitri must be saying that childhood

is the other side of the island, the place where
we grew up that is now so far away. Oh, but you

would be wrong. No, my friend, I am saying
where I come from is very far away.

Navigation

Even in this dry season, leaves grow
out of my heart on long vines.
No one believes me, but I can see them changing color.
I try to remember grasshoppers and fireflies
to prove I was once a child.
By the end of August the vines are covered
with dust. This frightens me almost as much
as my longing. When I am alone
two swallows fly by my window at sunset.
One, and only much later, another.
The sky goes blank without them.
At night I think about boats, the small *Skopelitis*
which took me to Donoussa and did not come back
until the storm was over. I sat with the Greeks
and watched the horizon, understanding finally
why they pray for fair winds. In ancient Greece
the ships never sailed straight out
to sea, they stayed close enough to always see
at least the edge of land.
Love gave me an island to keep in sight.
I navigated my small boat towards its shore.
When I cut the vines from my heart,
the sea rushed in immediately.

CHRISTOPHER BAKKEN

"If I am a poet, the air of Greece has made me one," Lord Byron said. I feel a similar debt, for I arrived on Greek soil with only the shallowest inkling of the way poetry could live in a landscape. I grew up in rural Wisconsin where archaeology consisted of Native American arrowheads in cornfields... that, or the local junkyard. The New World landscape has its species of hauntings, certainly, but I did not feel them as palpably as I did in a place like Greece, attended as it is by so many ghosts. Greece haunted me—it was there that I received my sensual and temporal education. The strata piled beneath my feet (Neolithic, Archaic, Hellenistic, Roman, Byzantine, Turkish, Nazi, etc.) were so deep they utterly bewildered and boggled any of my attempts to exhume fact from object or fiction. The house where I lived at Anatolia College once housed a Nazi officer when the Germans occupied Northern Greece (their headquarters consisted of the campus itself). There was the huge Nazi-bulldozed Jewish cemetery, the thirty-five thousand residents of Thessaloniki who were sent to Auschwitz. And there were the famous Byzantine churches with their dazzling mosaics; the edge of a Roman wall jutting out behind *souvlaki* shops in the middle of the modern city; and then the archaeological museum downtown with its golden amphorae from the tombs of Alexander's family.

Heidi Seibel

The poetic *problem* of Greece, then, was present in this daily embodiment. Words and place-names suggested too much there: Sparta, Thebes, Athens, Corinth. The Muses, those daughters of Mnemosyne, had to be resisted; memory in that landscape was almost too accessible, lying open to the elements everywhere in various states of ruin. Joseph Brodsky tells us that "there are places where history is inescapable, like a highway accident—places where geography provokes history." This was one of those places. As a result, in Greece I became obsessed with time; there I encountered the past, and it snorted like an animal at my back. Yet, that past was mostly inaccessible, unknown. I had to be satisfied with looking through artifacts, resting awhile in the ruined places that housed those artifacts—at Knossos, Delphi, Mycenae, Thebes—but also in the forgotten places I stepped without knowing it. In a landscape so full, it would not suffice to write travel poems, or any journalistic recording of places visited and objects seen, if only because Greece moved me so far beyond myself. How could I approach the present without drawing too much from the accidents of the ancient past? I asked my poetry in Greece to do what I could not sustain: to exist in the ancient and the modern present at the same time, in two worlds separated by so many centuries. The pursuit of a poetry that occupies both spaces at one time gave me a kind of necessary distance from both worlds and encouraged me to struggle to see from both perspectives, to sing of what endures.

Terra Incognita

Phaestos, 17th c. B.C.E.

Disc, you were buried so long we forgot
how to read: hieratic or hieroglyphic,
surely these doodads signify something.

From rim to center your brave little men
and large-breasted women leap backwards
among shields and beehive thingamabobs.

Who's chasing whom, where on earth, for what?
If only you were marble or hermatite,
you might be venerable, sacred: but clay?

Foundling of fires unwilling to speak,
you make, along with us, companion carbon,
a common corporation of dust.

Dion

In this way, every morning, all the houses smoke.
—Yiannis Ritsos

They rescued five goddesses this year,
    hauled from roots and mountain mud,
but today the men will wait before work,
    fat with hunger, while women fry onions

and *keftedakia* in the cramped kitchen.
　　By noon I'll join them, sweltering in pits,
peering my foreign eyes into their past
　　as we move earth and open it wider.

　　At Café Zeus Olympios, on this table
beneath a sagging trellis of grapes,
　　there's always one ashtray and some salt.
And somewhere, another mound to excavate
　　—brush, pick, sift-screen, barrow—
silt and strata of an imagined nation
　　buried at the outskirts of what we see,
where our digging borders the grain fields.

　　Here I believe in stone, existence in the flesh,
this cool libation in a galvanized pail:
　　water enough to rinse the urns and shard pile.
In the long pause before our feast begins,
　　the city beneath us constantly returns
and new tendrils unfurl from crowded vines;
　　silence blazes around the page where I write
since the earth is god I am not dust but god.

Alexandroupoli

When Yiannis drinks ouzo he falls asleep
uncounting a dingy twine loose strung
with variegated beads of glass,
his arthritic donkey tethered beside
the dank riverbed, gnawing nettles.
Minarets in fog sound beyond him
their five unorthodox agonies,
and generations of fishermen depart
in the same felt caps and odor of shellfish.
Dogs bark: women returning from market.
Everywhere the living are secure
as boundary stones dragged into the fields,
eroded, darkened by a faithful life's
undoing, pressed still between his fingertips.

Samothraki

Δεν ὑπάρχουν μάρτυρες πιά, γιά τίποτε
—Yiorgos Seferis

1

I took the ancient path from the silted harbor
to the Sanctuary, navigating fig groves,
stepping over barbed wire and donkey piles,
leaving my companions behind at the sea.
Separate signs in English and Greek tell
where the path leads: past the Anaktoron,
Hall of Lords, to altar court and fountain house.
The durable walls follow two cold streams
trickling down from the summit of Mt. Fengari.
Wandering in the Necropolis I found
stone lids of coffin-length stuck out from earth.
Below, in stale air, bones in urns are propped
for a lengthy drama, surrounded by votary
statues and jewels. Birds of fired clay tug
at the beveled corners of a tiny sarcophagus,
straining brittle wings to budge that weight.

2

They came across the Thracian Sea, braving
barbarians on land, then overcrowded boats;
in the cut and fill of waves freshly-painted eyes
blinked on their whitewashed prows. But here
sacrifice and sin leveled the faithful:
kings of Thebes and Macedonia had no privilege
over any other novice; Lysander came,
Herodotus, Alexander's parents met,
initiates among the fishermen and hogs.
For their arrival, trees were hung with masks,
village women gnawed raw flesh, announcing
with screams the god who appears. At the altar
of the Kabeiroi—those horny twins erected
as divine—human heads were wrapped in fine linen.
Most secrets of the mysteries have been well kept,
though in town today I believe I glimpsed

the Great Goddess herself, in sandals and rags,
peddling her thyme honey and barley rolls.

3

I'm led by hoof-prints to the weedy theatre,
sit awhile to drink in shade of a fallen column.
Something is missing from this mountainside,
in everyone who returns to Samothraki.
Branches sag without wind; the sea is calm.
With these stone stelea and pair of sacred streams,
the sanctuary retreats in one direction now.

The treasuries were plundered, are gone.
Winged Nike, whose chiton once crackled
in vicious winds, has gone from where she stood,
center of a still pool, as if perched to guide
an unsinkable ship; now she's landed for good
on a museum parapet in fluorescent light.

Where I walked today, a sign in all languages
once made it forbidden; but I went on through,
an intruder, stepping over the rough outline
of thresholds and walls. Immense black bees
followed me everywhere, lagging behind
to excavate the ubiquitous poppies.

4

Another road, I hoped, would lead somewhere,
descending hours in afternoon heat
to Pahia Ammos. I heard bells, protests
of the goats wearing them round their necks
grazing in rugged groves, or out of sight
in crags where no good shepherd ever
found a foothold. From below, on the beach,
mountain and sky seemed to exchange colors,
invisible springs showing up there as veins
of foliage, scattered blossoms spilled between
blank stone. Afternoons, while sun burns,
that same water relieves everyone coming
down from Profitis Ilias. By the battered fountain

young toughs lift weights in the shade, disputing
who is strongest, slamming ouzo and wine.

                    5

By way of the sun, or did they leave by sea?
We have their petrified grain and lopsided bowls;
their children played with knucklebones of beasts.
Even if we've missed them, these tumbled pillars
and sarcophagi exist, but no great gods will appear
to us, lost to all now alive, as voices are to me
inside those massive lidded graves. Feel the weight,
fill your pockets with sand, stand barefoot
in that burning light and still no one comes.
Walking back restores some mystery, stones,
a wall: enough to leave what is not there alone.

Zagora

When the room fills with sun I leave my poems,
        step to the balcony for cold coffee
and V.O.A. on the hotel's transistor.
        Some men have parked by the fountain
at the center of town: a farmer
        and his son, the village idiot,
who paces with a finger up his nose.
        Their rusted pick-up is packed with garlic,
a mountain of tidily braided skulls
        afire with gritty scents of Pelion.
Kyria Roula calls them with a wave.
        And, here, still balanced atop ladders,
paint-splattered Yiorgos and Socrates
        finish up another wall of whitewash.
I've taken their picture three times,
        not because they want to be remembered
by me, no, for their children, *ta paidia.*
        I could take another. They are perfect now.
But I'm thinking of the sea at Horefto,
        those palaces of octopus and marl,
far as I could walk from the tourists,
        from this village, its peninsula of stone,

where I spent the morning underwater
        chasing clouds of sepia ink,
the water's shadow, things that escape me.

Climbing Olympus, 1992

for Peter Balakian

What abyss
Was seen and passed over in silence.
—Czeslaw Milosz

The peak is not the peak? There's Mytikas,
just one hundred steep meters higher
than this jagged promontory: Skala,
staircase, where we stop at dawn to rest.
More cold and exhausted than in awe
of the mountain or the hawks circling above,
we are speechless, passing halvah, chocolate.

Last night's conversation was more lively,
fireside, fueled by a week-old article
in English: politics, policies, responsibility.
One empire scythed its bloody swath
from Diarbekir to Smyrna; another wants
to bandage Balkan sores with talk.
Someone broke a bottle in the end, invoked
Alexander, border wars, too much history.
Time wound up in the coals, exhaling
an eerie halo of phosphorescent greens.

At every step in the dark shale slipped
this morning, so only a few made it
beyond the tree line above Zolotas Lodge.
We climb on hands and feet like crabs at first
over the fog-licked stones, up the last crag,
then flattened against the wall, spread-eagled,
we creep past fissures where two Germans
were lost last fall, so near the summit.
Already the bravest among us, Anestis,
a somber Greek in army-issue fatigues,

has eased his way past the first chasm.
But he stops, shouts—δείτε—and we see,
crimson enveloping Athos to the east,
then burning harder to the north, Mt. Voras,
snow-lit and blinding on the border
of two Macedonias, the ancient and the new
republic. In the distance, still gray,
a froth of lesser peaks I do not know
to remember, and then, beyond them
somewhere almost unimaginable
are trucks hauling away too many men
in the first light, faces bewildered
by light in cities once called cities:
Gorazde   Sarajevo   Srebrenica

A. E. STALLINGS

It might surprise, but I am not very interested in ruins more recent than the Mycenaean age, nor even in much classical Greek art after the archaic. In a sense, if you've seen one Doric column, you literally have seen them all. Fifth-century Athens seems an irretrievably distant past to me. On the other hand, aspects of Homeric Greece sometimes feel as fresh as yesterday. There are scenes in modern Greece at almost no remove: The wildflowers and the country-side and the sea, the feast of lamb and bread and wine, words still in everyday parlance that were spoken by Achilles. Indeed, they still might be spoken by an Achilleas! I love where the contemporary and ancient rub shoulders with no sense of irony: the moving van labeled "Meta-phores"; the goatherd ushering home his goats from his Nissan pickup truck at the rising of Sappho's evening star, calling his wife Penelope on the cell phone. Here more than else-where you remember that all literature is, to the reader, contemporane-ous.

John Psaropoulos

A Postcard from Greece

Hatched from sleep, as we slipped out of orbit
Round a clothespin curve new-watered with the rain,
I saw the sea, the sky, as bright as pain,
That outer space through which we were to plummet.
No guardrails hemmed the road, no way to stop it,
The only warning, here and there, a shrine:
Some tended still, some antique and forgotten,
Empty of oil, but all were consecrated
To those who lost their wild race with the road

And sliced the tedious sea once, like a knife.
Somehow we struck an olive tree instead.
Our car stopped on the cliff's brow. Suddenly safe,
We clung together, shade to pagan shade,
Surprised by sunlight, air, this afterlife.

Apollo Takes Charge of His Muses

They sat there, nine women, much the same age,
The same poppy-red hair, and similar complexions
Freckling much the same in the summer glare,
The same bright eyes of green melting to blue
Melting to golden brown, they sat there,
Nine women, all of them very quiet, one,
Perhaps, was looking at her nails, one plaited
Her hair in narrow strands, one stared at a stone,
One let fall a mangled flower from her hands,
All nine of them very quiet, and one who spoke
Said, softly:

"Of course he was very charming, and he smiled,
Introduced himself and said he'd heard good things,
Shook hands all around, greeted us by name,
Assured us it would all be much the same,
Explained his policies, his few minor suggestions
Which we would please observe. He looked forward
To working with us. Wouldn't it be fun? Happy
To answer any questions. Any questions? But
None of us spoke or raised her hand, and questions
There were none; what has poetry to do with reason
Or the sun?"

The Wife of the Man of Many Wiles

Believe what you want to. Believe that I wove,
If you wish, twenty years, and waited, while you
Were knee-deep in blood, hip-deep in goddesses.

I've not much to show for twenty years' weaving—
I have but one half-finished cloth at the loom.
Perhaps it's the lengthy, meticulous grieving.

Explain how you want to. Believe I unravelled
At night what I stitched in the slow siesta,
How I kept them all waiting for me to finish,

The suitors, you call them. Believe what you want to.
Believe that they waited for me to finish,
Believe I beguiled them with nightly un-doings.

Believe what you want to. That they never touched me.
Believe your own stories, as you would have me do,
How you only survived by the wise infidelities.

Believe that each day you wrote me a letter
That never arrived. Kill all the damn suitors
If you think it will make you feel better.

An Ancient Dog Grave, Unearthed During Construction of the Athens Metro

It is not the curled up bones, nor even the grave
That stops me, but the blue beads on the collar
(Whose leather has long gone the way of hides)—
The ones to ward off evil. A careful master
Even now protects a favorite, just so.
But what evil could she suffer after death?
I picture the loyal companion, bereaved of her master,
Trotting the long, dark way that slopes to the river,
Nearly trampled by all the nations marching down,
One war after another, flood or famine,
Her paws sucked by the thick, caliginous mud,
Deep as her dewclaws, near the river bank.
In the press for the ferry, who will lift her into the boat?
Will she cower under the pier and be forgotten,
Forever howling and whimpering, tail tucked under?
What stranger pays her passage? Perhaps she swims,
Dogpaddling the current of oblivion.
A shake as she scrambles ashore sets the beads jingling.
And then, that last, tense moment—touching noses
Once, twice, three times, with unleashed Ceberus.

Aftershocks

We are not in the same place after all.
The only evidence of the disaster,
Mapping out across the bedroom wall,
Tiny cracks still fissuring the plaster—
A new cartography for us to master,
In whose legend we read where we are bound:
Terra infirma, a stranger land, and vaster.
Or have we always stood on shaky ground?
The moment keeps on happening: a sound.
The floor beneath us swings, a pendulum
That clocks the heart, the heart so tightly wound,
We fall mute, as when two lovers come
To the brink of the apology, and halt,
Each standing on the wrong side of the fault.

Athens, August

Even the days of the week have fled for the islands.
In the broken shadow of ruins, tourists huddle.
The citizens have vanished, melted away
In August's neutron bomb, its blinding silence.
A remnant of the faithful, at the bus stop,
Awaits the coming of the four-nineteen.
The pigeons mill through empty squares, at a loss.
No one heeds the prophesy of cicadas.
In dusty parks beneath the tattered palms,
Bareheaded statues cannot shade their eyes;
Stray dogs lap water from a leaking spigot.
As the sun reaches the height of absurdity,
A tree lets drop a single yellow leaf
To the pavement like a used bus ticket.

Minutes

Minutes swarm by, holding their dirty hands out,
Begging change, loose coins of your spare attention.
No one has the currency for them always;
Most go unnoticed.

Some are selling packets of paper tissues,
Some sell thyme they found growing wild on hillsides,
Some will offer shreds of accordion music,
Sad and nostalgic.

Some have only cards with implausible stories,
Badly spelled in rickety, limping letters,
"Help me—deaf, etcetera—one of seven
Brothers and sisters."

Others still accost the conspicuous lovers,
Plying flowers looted from cemeteries,
Buds already wilting, though filched from Tuesday's
Sumptuous funeral.

Who's to say which one of them finally snags you,
One you will remember from all that pass you,
One that makes you fish through your cluttered pockets,
Costing you something:

Maybe it's the girl with the funeral roses,
Five more left, her last, and you buy the whole lot,
Watching her run skipping away, work over,
Into the darkness;

Maybe it's the boy with the flute he fashioned
Out of plastic straws, and his strident singing,
Snatches from a melody in a language
No one can teach you.

CHARLES FISHMAN

My visit to Greece in the summer of 1995 deepened my feeling for place and history. Long
after I returned to the States, images of my
journey through Greece—her beauty and her
mystery—continued to haunt me, pushing me
to capture that visual and sensual trajectory in
words. My new manuscript, *Country of Memory*
(2004), will include a sequence of poems written in Greece or within the two years after my
return. I expect to write more.

Andros Night

for D.S.

Darkness came up, so we walked
into town. An old woman had shown us
the short-cut: through the wood that opened
below the village, along the small turbulence
of the creek—just keep to the path and we'd be safe.
Night settled around us, but we found the road,
and the lights on the coast awoke.

Later, we met other travelers, ate with them
and drank. Simple food, good wine, and talk of home—
what could be sweeter? Someone—perhaps you, my friend—
bought another round. A bouzouki played in the distance
and the shore of the island swayed. Sweet fellowship
of the night breeze and the bottle! I think we sang
the anthem of lost brothers.

Then we headed back toward the village and the lights
of the town blew out. We walked slowly upwards,
talked of poetry and love. The stars circled above us.

But the secret path, this night, would remain a secret,
the entrance hidden in the Andros dark. To be truly lost
—that would be romantic! What great poets we would be,
if we could drift between the worlds: poet-angels, whose words
would have the brightness of comets.

But, this night, we were merely lost: the empty white churches
and their cobalt cupolas did not waken, nor did the roadside shrines
glisten as we stepped through starlight, bound to this earthly
plane. Here is where we would labor over our lines and here
we'd caress all we loved. We were lost in Andros night.
We circled upwards. The breeze of an old darkness chilled us.

The Light at Ligourio

for Dimitrios Smirlis

In the arbor at Ligourio, grapes grow round
with sun and, under the sun-drunk grapes,
a family I love clusters: my friend, Dimitrios,
my dark-eyed student once; his mother, earthy
and true as Ligourio wine; his father, temperate
in the face of bureaucrats and weather.

Time has ripened them to silence, or nearly so.
Each day, they waken to sun, to the musk of sun-
drenched flowers. Time drifts more slowly, olive trees
steep in the dusty heat of July. At Ligourio, life
is not a dream: this family thrives beneath the grapes
that grow round and fragrant.

They ripen with the grapes that cluster above them:
you can see how they breathe here, where quiet
shadows sweep the hand-hewn stones and white
armfuls of stars gather, as on a trellised vine that winds
through the arboreal galaxies: as on a vine that stems
from the source of darkness and delight.

MOIRA EGAN

Among the many things I'll never forget about my three years in Greece are the sunsets. From my balcony on a steep hill above Thessaloniki, I had a perfect view of the Thermaic Gulf, and on clear days I could even see Mount Olympus. On very clear days, I could see the etchings in the snowcaps of that mythic mountain. I began to understand theogony. During my first week in Greece, I saw the most awe-inspiring sunset ever. In fact, it makes a cameo appearance in one of my poems: "Alchemical sunsets hammer gold / from lead, the rays even redder / than the madder of a family drama." Such violent beauty led me to thoughts of how those ancient Greeks came to invent their gods— or is it that they just saw them more clearly? I would rush back to my flat after school so as not to miss that day's sunset. It wasn't just me; in the lovely town of Oia on Santorini, tourists gather every evening to watch the sun pass below the horizon, and when the last hot-orange drops are squeezed into the sea, the "audience" applauds. I saw the gods, yes.

Studio Fotografia Pappou-Evangelidi

I lived in Greece during NATO's bombing of Kosovo, about one hundred fifty miles up the road from Thessaloniki, which has seen its own share of history, war, ethnic cleansing. Just up the road, NATO dropped bombs containing depleted uranium. The first rain after the bombing came down upon us acid and purple. I am not exaggerating; I was caught out in it without an umbrella, and the rain burned my face. For months the sunsets were violent: blood red, scar pink, vicious purple. Greece's landscape, ageless as it is, bears the marks of its history.

Liminal Hymn

(for Alicia Stallings and Bob Clawson)

I know a man who wants to know the very hour
when bats replace the tracings of swallows
in the sky, when sonar echoes flowers,
sight's subsumed by ways of knowing

light-forgotten. Listen: that moan you hear
could be the farewell of a fisherman's boat,
the ghost you tried to leave behind, who's here,
or Athena's owl waking, clearing her throat.

This is not the hour for asking questions.
Feel the moon rise, her diaphanous robe
taking substance from her brother, the sun,
who turns away, slightly envious, cloak

slung over shoulder beside Reason and Truth.
In in-between time, mysteries undim,
the sea calms, cools to anemone blue.
This is the hour when the pale women swim.

Dear Mr. Merrill,

I hope you'll pardon the informality
of this letter, postmarked Olympia
(Greece, not Washington), its task not simple:
crossing lines you've crossed, time, mortality,
to find you, who spent a lifetime crossing lines
out, twisting, polishing them to shine

cool and lustrous as the statue I fell in
love with yesterday. I'm sure you saw him
too, that perfect Hermes by Praxitelis,
full lips, hips *contrapposto*. I wished to draw him
down, latter-day Pygmalion, and embrace
him. Or barring Eros (and the guards) I'd trace

his face, the supple muscle of the marble.
I had a student who resembled him—
yes, Angelos—arrogant and beautiful.
I never touched him though he touches me in dreams.
Eros dangles his perfection in our faces
like one-armed Hermes with his promise of the grapes.

I was certain I'd dream of him last night.
Instead I dreamed another in the growing chain
of others with whom it ended not quite
right. But the thirst was perfect, if its price pain
and shattered crystal, spilling wine, all part
and parcel of our imperfect lives. Then Art

startles out of heart ache, marble or page.
You learned this long ago. Now I too see
the wildest things require the strongest cages,
the panther's double bars, or the seeds,
bloodysweet and bitter, in the pomegranate's
rind. Love held tight in a sonnet.

MARK SARGENT

In Portland, Oregon, I was content to be a local poet. I edited and published small magazines and performed my work, most often in collaboration with other poets and artists, at galleries, taverns and universities, on street corners, and sometimes with my own free jazz band. I had a good time roaming about the city ruffling feathers and being loud. But a poetry career—a Master of Fine Arts degree, national publications, fellowships, teaching positions—held no interest.

Nancy Wheaton

In 1990 when I moved with wife and child to a small village in the mountains above Sparti, I was artistically utterly alone—without a local community, artistic or otherwise—and to be heard at all required pushing my work out beyond where I could see. Having moved from a city to the country, my focus turned as well to the natural world at hand. Struck by a landscape that spoke a human language, I went back to ancient Greek texts as a way of translating what I heard. No longer performing my work required me to refocus my attention on the sound created on the page, on the white where poetry that lasts has always dwelt. What followed was a shortened breath line and a pared-down language that felt more international, less American, while retaining its roots in the Pound/ Olson tradition. Being without a community of peers gave me the freedom to experiment with traditional forms, something I might not have done had I remained in the States. I always had wanted a way out of America, and then I met a woman who said, "Come with me to Greece." I did, and a poetry career is just as far away as ever.

In the Dark Noise of the Olive Press
Young Men Work and Old Men Watch

A dozen machines roar
while we mill about drinking wine
smoking, watching the green
ooze and flow from grinding wheel
to churning vat, paste on the mats
piled high and squeezed slow.

The countryside needs
thick young men
to man the machinery
push things around
grunt and smoke
feed the world.

I am one of the men who watch
who stand and pace along the machines
when it's their olives being pressed.
A generation ago I was filthy
and dense, pushing to keep up
taking ladders at a run
and dumb, not much thinking
when you work that hard
just keep your head down
till the harvest is done.

I hope those young guys
are getting more than
I think they are. Muscle
doesn't pay you squat
these days, even here
where it's needed the most.

Yet it feels good to be
that hard, able to push past
the little wheels of brain
to the grease and brawn
of manufacturing
the great dark noise
thick as oil curls 'round muscle

and pulls you down
to the throb and pulse
hump and groan insatiability
of power brought
to motor and steel.

This work,
your pay is counted out
in your hand
fits in your pocket
buys a real good time.

In the Weather

for Susan Howard

Seeing me regularly
in the hills with
my stick and dog
the locals must think:
Why doesn't he just get
some goats and make
himself useful?
            Too easy.
Too hard. Too...
well, much with
the grain.
            I walk
in order to get
a better angle
on the sky.
            Tonight
a moon six days full,
Venus lingering above
Lazeenikos, dark full
of bleating screams
returning sheep
dog bark shepherd whistle
bell clang and clatter
                  I work
my way down

through the olives,
light as the moon
and far away,
useful as stone.

Watching a Storm's Aftermath Without Regret

In the wake of lightning and thunder a drizzly grey
hangs over the valley a pissy *if only* mist drifts
across the hills like lonely longings for the past.
A lot of this goes on, people enter the weather
of the day and drip out transformed memory
and muscle and heart where there wasn't any.
I had met Melita and we were gathering steam
when one day I entered my house to find a note
that Szabo, an old lover had phoned, was in town
could we, perhaps. And I sat, looked at the note
and heard her voice, smelled her and figured
that a wild night on the town could easily ensue
punctuated by crazed drunken fucking into
the wee hours or later but at some point the sun
would shine on the whole affair and what was
always there would still be there and we would part
glad of our union and sure that it was only made
for gypsy moments shouted into the heaving dark.
That night the woman who would be my wife made
long love to me that in the light of day revealed
more there than was before, a crack of light a glimpse
warm wash of liquid air a passage into time expanded
that has led to this wet day I am allowed to see
as flux of atmosphere complete with friendly spirits
floating past those humping waves of olive.
Goodbye ghosts, and come again,
I know your names and won't forget.

DIANE THIEL

Although I have always felt a connection with the incredibly rich history and mythology of Greece, my personal relationship with the country has been a vital part of my writing life. My  husband, Costa, is a Greek citizen, though he has lived in the United States for a number of years, and with him I have seen not only many back roads and quiet villages, but have had more than a window into everyday Greek life.

Though the family lives primarily in northern Greece (Macedonia), we have spent extended periods of time in a number of other regions as well: the Athens area, Peloponnese (including the Mani), Crete, and several Aegean islands. We also have spent time in other parts of the world that are culturally and/or ethnically Greek, or that have intriguing links with Greek history. My husband and I were married on the island of Cyprus. And one of the reasons I chose to be in Odessa, on the Black Sea, as a Fulbright Scholar is the region's fascinating links to Greek history, from ancient to contemporary times. We took an ancient route to arrive there, from Greece to Istanbul, and then through the Bosporus and across the Black Sea to Odessa. The Black Sea hosts many ancient outposts, such as Olbia and Yalta, the latter having received its legendary name from the Greek sailor's cry, *yalos* (shore), upon sighting land after many days lost at sea in a storm.

These influences have found their way into my work in both direct and indirect ways. Mythology takes on a different dimension in my writing, perhaps, as a myth might be linked to an actual photograph of a relative, as in "Daphne (A Photograph, 1930)." In "Legacy" the story of Icarus becomes linked with the tragic death of J.F.K. Jr., which I heard news of while on the island of Aegina.

The trials of entering a new language via one's domestic life also have figured in my work in indirect ways. In a poem in which I discuss my mother's entry (after marrying my father) into a new language, German, I allude to the realization that my own entry into Greek language and marriage helped give rise to the poem about her experience.

164

The more recent (twentieth-century) historical issues in Greece—dislocation, war, and civil strife—are subjects I have written about in various ways. A major focus of much of my work has been the exploration of the effects of war on future generations. Issues of dislocation and loss of a homeland are keen ones, particularly for the people of the region of Macedonia. Discussions with my family in Greece have helped to shape this choice of subject matter, even when I write about dislocation elsewhere in the world.

Legacy

(for J.F.K. Jr. 1960–1999)

Aegina—waking to the news on the radio
in Greek, so fast all I hear is your name
again and again—that terrible tone.
The long day's pause—awaiting confirmation.
How could we not collectively think
of a curse on your house? On Greek TV,
I see the photos of your childhood
framed by your father's desk and casket.
Across the ocean, Peruvians submerge
the pictures in the river to cleanse your name.
You seemed to be emerging from the hollows
of this century, somehow unscathed—Still,
you sought the skies' escape, like Icarus,
Phaethon, so many legendary children.
It was the legacy you couldn't trade
that brought you everything too early on—
a changeling sent at three into the sun.

Daphne (A Photograph, 1930)

I know, in that moment caught, how she was fleeing—
her face eternally still, her body taut,
training every tendril of her being,
holding her in place—the raised knot

of her face eternally still, her body taught
by years of silence, that straight upper lip

holding her in place—the raised knot
of an old laurel tree, the tightening grip

of years of silence—that straight upper lip
we remember so much from the past. Poised, she stands
like an old laurel tree—the tightening grip
of that long summer falling like earth through her hands.

We remember so much from the past. Posed, she stands
by that field where she fell, her face in the hot grain
of that long summer, falling to Earth with her hands.
She would grind by stone and eat the seeds again

by that field where she fell, her face in the hot grain,
her mouth still. Closed. No one would see the swell
she would grind by stone—and eat the seeds again
that next Sunday at the cool garden table.

Her mouth still closed. No one would see the swell,
training every tendril of her being,
that next Sunday, at the cool garden table.
I know, in that moment caught, how she was fleeing.

Event Horizons

Swallow

It may take one
tiny hollowed skeleton
on the stoop below—
for the eyes to rise and see
the swallows nesting
beneath the window.

Silences

In a small boat, the world
becomes big and wild again.
The weather is more than words,

but what you live your life by—
that loneliness you can touch
like a smooth tree you know,

but don't know the name of.

Thera

Why do we want to go
to the rim of that volcano
that spelled oblivion—
to lift her layered, dark hem
and touch the city lost again
beneath a wine-dark ocean?

Circumstance

If she was recognized, she turned herself
into a tree, grew stories from her fingertips,
shook them off like bright, gold leaves in the wind.
Or she held them heavy, offered the fruit
for a new life—within inches, or miles,

if the right bird was there at the right time.

Her trees traveled in the bellies of birds,
flew great distances, allowed circumstance
of wind, of rain, of storm, of flight, or fire
to do the planting, place them in the ground,
in the dark soil of her ancestors.

CHARLES O. HARTMAN

My first encounter with Greece in 1997, at the late age of forty-eight, was above all an encounter with Greek. I arrived knowing none, plunged in,

learned too little too slowly, but to my own surprise began constructing poems in this language of the passionate lexicon and perspicuous structure. After that quick semester and a dozen poems, I was able to return for a little longer stay in 1999. But instead of more poems in Greek I found myself building a long English poem about walking in Greece: a 2,400-digit pi-mnemonic that traces a daylong walk around and then over the island of Aegina (which is triangular, not round, but mythos has its perquisites). Shortly afterward I spent three weeks writing poems (about seventy) as fast as I could, catalyzing the details and rhythms of Greek shores, stories, villages, and weathers. All of these poems, from Greece and Greek, will make up a book called *Island*. I had never lived on one before.

Now in late 2002 I'm back once again, trying more seriously to come to terms with the language and the vocal culture as a medium of talk, as well as of absurdly meticulous construction. Greece offers a bounty, unparalleled in my experience, of poems for the writing, and it is very hard for me to know how much of this is due to simple foreignness, how much to the palpably sentient scrutiny of the light, how much to the reverberations of history in every stone and greeting. I don't believe I could live here, for the intensity of influx; but I am coming to spend my time away from Greece scheming how to return.

from "Tambourine"

Also, he made a molten sea of ten cubits from
brim to brim, round in compass...and a line
of thirty cubits did compass it round about.
—2 Chronicles 4:2

Now:

I walk a coast brilliant as dragon glass
    for water flinging splinters chaotic alongside
        and in the distance long orders of island
            spun for the occasion out of morning
                corporeal light

As mythical violence sets a bloodline running
    a cooler intention now
        austerely furnishes the horizon broad O

Light examines me

Isometric leaning wind
    beatifies this mind
        grown credulous as air

Vagrant entirely
    I borrow time

Giving in
    finesses giving up

Electing something devouring
    finesses giving up
        superbly

Now this universe at large has lost an I
    I
        locates

Seeing invents
    otherwise anywhere
        is a same nonplace

Nonsense errant
    makes a bid to submerge it all

Tumult seiges each boulder

Assiduous its breakers
    maul each island

Buggerall stops still

Three quarters of an age
    I devoted to sloth and worry
        nearabout dead

Whenever I do halfwise
    that dreadful I O U
        closely held
            grows

No rockdove says I

No pelican

A cumbrance
    for voyagers
        lined in a V

Being human makes traveling
    harder with some reason
        if it compounds with becoming
            pleasures worth
                just traveling for

The variable I
    rehearses values
        that like to approach constant X

Character happens while selves attend other urgencies
    and the form that unseen X is
        intuited from vividly drawn dreams
            mind projects on the odd daytime seascape
                barely noticed produces
                    the I Steady Stand
                      or phantom I am

X
    saturates

Meanwhile I walk miles graced
    with circling gulls
        storks lofted
            garnering
                of the very island

The very searocks exhale X

Most truth lies
    but in strict rhythm lies
        accuracy in a way
            now arbitrary
                now direct

Measure in action

So this metrician
    X says I am
        squares the spheres
          we hear
            every footfall
                centers

---------- 0 ----------

Echoes return

Inland for a sight
    climb passages
        reciting a history
            each mountain bespeaks a piece of

Orogenies do

Narrative yearns
    to continue
        as geography
          is never done

Expansion a century a digit
    has charms even the wholly frantic
        educated gradually to
            might apprehend

Not simply

---------- 0 ----------

X
       I say
              can

Rocks may

Water says
       counting enchants it

Each figure trains waves to a new hypnotic ease I have
       copied painfully
              while I confirmed
                     when I seize X
                            X eludes

Cuchulain
       hews the sea

Waves
       trouble at nothing

Yet taking scant thought
       water
              toothless
                     gnaws senseless a shoreline
                            rawly new

Possessed of a brainpan
       facing X
              I blinked
                     yes
                            grasping a mischance for it
                                   facing X I forbore
                                          mymisself and I

Known X
       I imagined
              would lose vitality

Suppose that this heresy be now finally abandoned
      supposing dinner is frankly more startling after having
           starved for years a hopeless abnegant quite tightly
                woven in weblets of self dominion espousing
                    a by no stretch universal law
                      relieved
                          I remember now

I a patchwork from wayonback
      I an epiphenom emergent
           for the moment
                compact for the moment am
                hard work

Suited labor charms
      fervor
           past due

Peripaty counts

As a day convolves
      this clockwise pace around the perimeter
           turns on an edgy craving for mastery
                I recognize

Roaming

As a century convolves
      peramble counts

Songlines
      tune
           the travels

So rhythms thicken

Timed for walkabout by a skysign
      I measure myself by milestone for a roadway
           sandal leather takes on the waywiser
                with nearly nothing left unproven I discover
                    this merely walking making living
                      seriously
                        fine

Mused
　　I say so

　　---------- 0 – 0 ----------

Blood struts lordlier
　　I do believe
　　　　a body given to taking
　　　　　　joy where bidden

Fortunes in delight pervade anyplace sense awakens
　　example
　　　　a guy with an octopus
　　　　　　turns seawall
　　　　　　　　through thorough thwacking
　　　　　　　　tender

Elsewhere
　　a rooster too dimwit for morning I suppose
　　　　blithely hollers at a blue heaven overhead
　　　　lust loud

Splendoes

I am an eary gathering
　　quiet
　　　　and loud too

A boat passes
　　laden with wayfarers
　　　　steam sounding forth his initial O

Oomph

Echoing pulsation of an echoing pulsation
　　voices vitulate broadcast
　　　　on every timeworn frequency
　　　　　　to get their word in

A helpfully undefined limit
　　namely I
　　　　f of X
　　　　　　am listening

So a quodlibet
        begins

Creation
        pushes back

The next cape I navigate
        a coast brilliant etcetera
                a new manner of arranging reality
                        repeats that nothing
                                masters a day

Impatient
        prodigity rounds

Wryly
        a fraction escapes

Mindful of X
        I set down whichever dimension
                whichever magnitude
                        whichever direction suggests the vectors
                                of veritably pilgrim progress

Most theolatry bullshits about X

Since doctrinal middens are a pitfall
        out of courtesy
                X eludes

Hindsight
        traces out
                a rambling
                        bound
                                territory round

It maps
        this value beginning with
                three point one four
                        wooing expansion

Fabulous day

An ardent toil of
    prowl it is
       too

Plenties of hours
    and for each word
       twenty trancing steps

The heart is speech
    a perimeter
       and I
           a rational diameter
            I address X

O

      ---------- 0 – 0 ----------

And I can compass stepping out
    sideways without being an untoward outaline
       faring paths
          findable between wants
         and has to

Wherever
    and whenever I need to

Behind a hillock
    a further hillock arises
       series
          extending I feel
            endless and

Not right naturally
    interior is bound and thus
       reachable

Just as Odyssean cursive trips trace some Aegean bestiary
      showing how a π might designate
           areas easily as limiting curves for circular thinking
              so the lines any venture overland between hills
                describes all meander along a
                    sleepwalk never seeming Ithacan
                      spelling a babbling drawl
                        tending finally
                          homeward

After all
    if I signify
        I do it before thinking

Chance
    choose a way

      ---------- 0 ----------

A humdinger
    of another stairway
        notated mutely
            begins C D E
                ascending
                    agile intervals

Logarithm of a scalar
    step
        up

A monotonic goatbell
    somewhere off
            confirms

Harmonial
    scads of birds
        entitle me

I

Beyond where this hillside climb declines
          giving way to gentler geodesic tangents
               beyond where indulging the sloped
                    a craze
                         has had setbacks
                              I plodding or lightly
                                   gravitate toward
                                        desiring to fly

How

I delectate
     going to

And going too

A peculiar piece of highblown rustic rhetoric ricochets aimlessly about various
          heights the better to be heard overabove headwinds that a sun stiffens
               hazarding a no less fruitless descent to a muddled echoing depth
                    to validate the most fuckwit theophany I ken
                         a dance I dance
                              quite elegant with practice
                              quite regular
                                   to walk to talk
                                        being
                                             what I heard

Memory
     producing music
          reabsorbs music

Fanfares no orchestra belts out
     and I a player
          resonate around a network of earshot
               focusing every nerve
                    rewarded
                         spirally receptive

Valleys
     sound

Listening minutely for
          instance I saunter
                along this saddle
                      all yawning ears
                            noting what melodizes the formulary
                                  for X
                                        economies of scale aside

Stride

Rite

                ---------- 0 ----------

Attention
          is telling
                measure

A needle
          seeking X
                I pay attention

                ---------- 0 ----------

Villagers populate this rambling
          abruptly
                in kind

I go fumbling
          among palatals and velars
                a barbar

Old women darken
          the benches

Donkeys
          loudly abound

O

They radiate X

P. H. LIOTTA

As for the intensely personal issue of "What is my relationship to Greece?"—how best to answer the unanswerable? My roots, of course, are

Donna Liotta

Macedonian, and I can trace my family origins back three thousand years to the Doric invasion of Sicily. (Our surname stems from *eliotis*—the machine used to press olives in making oil.) But I have to admit, despite having lived and worked in Yugoslavia in the late 1980s, nothing truly prepared us for our life in Greece from 1993 to 1996. In many ways I was living in the most enchanting part of Europe, yet I also found Athens to be one of the most difficult and challenging locations in the Mediterranean. This tension, I hope, comes through in my poems. As I was working as a military diplomat in Athens, I was under a direct assassination threat from the 17 November terrorist group (now an organization that is only a bad memory). I recall one morning when we had already moved three times during our first year living in Greece. I stood holding my daughter, Gaia, on our terraced balcony in the community of Politea, north of Athens. I had been working on a manuscript for several years about the Balkans and had known I wanted the title to come from Beethoven's chorale, "The Ruins of Athens." This happened a few days after 17 November assassinated a young businessman in broad daylight in central Athens. I kept thinking, *It could be you....* And, of course, it could have been; but the slow sense of creeping terror and constant dread perhaps perversely left me with an ever-deeper love for family and things to be cherished. So, to be honest, I have always measured my life as "before" and "after" Greece.

The Language of Angels

The children of Bosnia are on again tonight,
though the performance is the last, I think,
to trouble their mortal sleep. But the man

with the bad toupee draws deep on his filterless
cigarette, leans into history, and in hoarse
torrents of Greek tells us what we must do,
what numbers to call. Then the montage
of twisted limbs and blood, by now the standard
images of ruin I will never understand.
A tiny waif in her pink tutu floats past
the television monitors, arms coupled
in the arch of peace and friendship. *It's up
to the angels now,* he exclaims. *And to you.*

And it's true. But by now, I've had enough. I turn
away and Gaia turns to me for explanation.
I wish I knew. The Caravan of Hope, with the orphans
of Sarajevo on board, had come to Salonica for seven nights
at Christmas. And tonight the Epiphany arrives,
when the three men were guided by the star, when
the angel spoke to them and they understood.
But for the children of Bosnia, it's not so simple.
Tomorrow they return to Sarajevo, to all that
madness. No one here will take them.
Already there are tales of breaking loose, Byzantine
whispers that the Caravan of Hope is heading south
to the wine-dark Aegean and will not stop

until they arrive in Crete or head farther south,
to Libya, Land of Lotus Eaters, until they find
someone who will understand, someone who will take them in,
tell them it no longer matters, that *here* is a place
to let you grow and a time that wants you.
What seems so simple…how nothing ever is.
                    And then the ring at the door,
outside in the street, beyond the walls of our locked gate.
The Children of Bosnia are here and we have to
let them in, have to give them something warm
and lasting while they tell the story of their lives.
Gaia and Donna and I will move among them,
bring them to a house suddenly large,

where room after room appears we never knew
existed. And Gaia, who speaks with the voice of an angel,
all music and light, will hold each one

in her embrace, and proclaim *You are my best friend*...
Here is Gjoko, son of Danko—who was my first Croation
teacher and who is now no longer, another
martyr of Mostar. The boy has his father's eyes,
dark and luminous, that question everyone.
Here is Slobodna, whose name means freedom,
who cannot speak and will not make a sound for months.
Naïma, Branko, Goran...they stretch off like a hall of mirrors.
Suddenly, around the fire, we converse in a tongue none
of us seems sure of. But we believe it could happen.

This is the night when miracles occur. They say
the animals knelt before the power that they felt,
and the three ancient men were blinded by the star
yet followed because there was something in the voice
that spoke to them, something that *seemed* true.
So it could be. Donna has placed a blanket on the shoulders
of those who still shiver and are afraid. *No need to worry.*
I give them a drink named Απάτη Θανάτου—
The Trick of Death—that comes from villages high on
the slopes of Taïyetos. And it seems true, since tricking death
and life are the only things to get us by, when we have to
believe what's here, as we fall through this universe
together, at the same eternal speed, this same blinding fury.

Somewhere an angel has opened her wings.
Somewhere a country true enough to hold.
Somewhere a hearth that has always been waiting,
with a fire warmed by the victims of chance, where
the goddess of mourning bends to her loom, weaving
a myth about mystery and fate in the language of loss.
Somebody loves us all.

Politeia, Athinai

The True Colours of Ikons

are smoke and flame, the mediums of faith
—cast upon the water as the water's mirror—
the argosies of dust, trued by light:
spirit rising from the matter that is form.

Cast upon the water as the water's mirror,
a body of work the sole body of thought.
Spirit rising from the matter that is form.
The language, what passes over into silence

—a body of work the sole body of thought—
a sentence we may never speak.
This, language? What passes over into silence,
whatever takes us from the fire, where

a sentence we may never speak
will turn upon our words that meant resolve.
Whatever takes us from the fire, where
every step is a letter and every path

will turn upon your words that meant resolve.
God in the abyss of every dream:
Every step is a letter and every path
a sentence handed down as prayer.

God in the abyss of every dream,
or word, since words are always failures
—a sentence handed down as prayer—
faith peregrined from reverence and torment.

Or word, since words are always failures
of the hidden, a trader doubly burdened,
faith peregrined from reverence and torment,
commencing from one stillness to another

of the hidden, a trader doubly burdened:
in running water; as well, the sleep of stones.
Commercing from one stillness to another,
the seed of sleep enciphering the script.

In running water—as well, the sleep of stones—
the argosy of dust, trued by light.
The seeds of sleep, enciphering the script,
are smoke and flame, the mediums of faith.

Xenophontos, Mount Athos

Man with a Kite

Somewhere near the middle passage of a sort of life,
a man takes up his oars and rows from the wood.
He considers, as the blades skim and dip, a mirror
of absence, how it might show him something that mattered, some fire
that burns through his core, leads him astray.
He begins thinking of kites, and the language of angels.

Because in the end, if it were anything, it was angels
he was meaning to find, some luminous spirit or life
to show how he had to come so far astray.
He holds up the kite to the wind, hoping the wood
will hold in the strain of the wind, the way the fire
inside him portrays, if he looks closely enough, the mirror

of his own private agonies, those mysteries a mirror
of who he's become, how far from the idea of angels
he's travelled; closer now to that other place, its eternal fire.
At least, once, he'd believed in these things, in some other life.
Now, the cartoon face of a mouse on a kite flies high over the wood.
He seems tethered to it, to keep from drifting astray.

Still, moving in a current of stillness, he feels like a stray,
the refuge of some great disaster. He looks to the edge, into the mirror
the black water shows him: he sees a man with a face made of wood.
What would they say of me now, my guardian angels?
he asks the mouse on the kite. *A life
formed by the love of a wife and a daughter,* and a fire

inside which came from the source of all fire.
There, high above, the mickey mouse kite turning astray.
He reels it back down, holding the life
that springs from its flight from the earth. It was a mirror,
of course—he, who wanted to fly with the angels.
He had been born with wings made of wood.

Comes a cry, piercing and anguished, out of the dark wood,
something that sings, deeply, like the tongue of fire
against flesh, in the moment when none of the angels
can save you, when you are left to stray

for yourself, to find yourself in the mirror,
to say to yourself: *That was my life.*

And what is this imperfect wilderness, this stray wood? A mirror
of the street torment of earth, the runes of angels—whatever rises
from the fire, these ruins out of which you make a life.

Delphi, Parnasos

A Prayer for My Daughter

<<*Ταξιδεύουμε πάντα με τον Χάρων στο πλευρό μας*>>
We travel always with Charon at our side
—saying among Greek fishermen

Skimming the surface beneath shadow and dream,
    the voice of my daughter trails from the dark
to reach from the room beside us. Once more a storm
    is howling, and half-alive I pray for sleep, for peace.
Awake already an hour, the ocean of blood in my ears
    throws back these unrelenting fears, these past lives
eager to consume me. And Gaia, child of Chaos and Time,
    wife of the Sky, mother of Gods, the very Earth herself—
my daughter—her cries are real and I do nothing but pray
    for sleep—not even two yet, she cries with the voice of a woman
who knew nothing but sorrow or loss—and now her plea *Daddy,*
    where are you? shows how it's never too early
for the nature of grief. I think of the day a few weeks ago
    I held the last shudder of our dog Shakespeare in my arms
and felt him let go, knew it was real the way he looked to us to say
    he knew what love was, real the way I cried with a sense that
nothing matters, nothing at all, I don't care, the way our
    friend Yanni lies in a bed in the dark now, our friend who is
turning away, turning to light, becoming the person no one
    remembers. He will be dead by Christmas. Only this morning
you, Gaia, danced about our dining table, about his tree of
    memory, made with the care of your mother's hands, its
green branches sealed with felt red Möbius strips cut at one
    end, as if to show the soul the way of escape, the way you
will travel to the riverbank and take the coin you were given
    at death to the one who stands in the boat over water, the
one who will take you forever. From the first when I leaned
    over the bars of your crib and saw who I was, from the day

P. H. LIOTTA   185

you remembered the smell of my body, the touch when I held
     you more to save myself than ever out of cause to rescue you,
we were connected, from need as much as loss. Each day I
     grow older, though not in wisdom exactly but the best I can do.
Each night I return from the habitual murder of language
     by bureaucrats to the dancing music of words, the voice of my
daughter, the voice of your tongue and your babble of speech, a
     brook of clear water. Only then I believe. And how could you
know what you'll inherit? The blood of Alexander runs in our
     past, and for three thousand years the truth of our race
has been the tribute of blood—a river of ash—from the day
     it started at Grancius and the one the Persians named "that
drunken lout who sacked Persepolis" believed it was possible
     to go beyond God, to be more than a God, even after the tenth
philosopher told him, in answering his question on whether
     death was stronger than life, that "life remains strongest,
because it supports so many miseries," until it ended
     when the Macedonian destroyer of men commanded the city
of Susa to be "dealt by the sword" and the glint of their spears flared
     in the light and every last bone of each living thing turned
into dust. The fire of rage and a temple of anger are the truths
     that run in my veins, though it is the threnody of love I have
always thirsted for. Deep, inside, the breath of a last survivor
     will taunt me. If only women ruled the earth, my daughter,
it would be the right place for love. But they don't and it's right
     only out of loving to spite the truth. And when I wake
to the surface from sleep it is your voice that will save me, your
     life and all that you give, even the taut whip of anger
that becomes an inheritance, the flare of becoming whatever you see:
     my own father leaning back into me, telling me how *you'll never*
be anything more... and whoever lays a head to your breast, years
     from now, will hear me inside you, whispering anger and hatred
and love, the course of our histories like lines, like rivers, saying
     our stories make sense only as much as our lives. Yes,
in dream, I emerge and feel the terrible angel trailing
     beneath me, the weight of a naked heart in my hands.
And when you come to the surface, Gaia, I pray you will know
     how love must carry me with you, carry me with you

for ever: All that we were, all we will ever be.

Beograd-Skopje-
Bucureşti-Athinai

186   P. H. LIOTTA

REBECCA NEWTH

I was in Greece in 1994–95 on Crete where the University of Crete Arts and Humanities Division is located. My husband, a librarian at Yale and the University of Arkansas, acted as a consultant to the fledgling library, at that time housed in a high school in Rethymno, now at home in its permanent site near Gallou, overlooking the sea. I wrote in the library while my husband worked with the librarians and staff. The impact of being in Greece—from the moment I boarded an Olympic Airlines plane with Greek lettering on its side, to using the Greek computer site "Zeus"—was immensely suggestive of all that Western civilization has to offer. I wrote thousands of words while staying for our month-long sabbatical and visited everywhere I could on Crete, from the sometimes inaccessible south shore to the historic Minoan sites in the North. One of my current writing projects involves a privately owned Renaissance Venetian garden near Chania, a garden that has obsessed me since 1995 and that I plan to revisit during 2003 in order to finish the book.

Andrew Kilgore

House of Sky

Prophecy, the form of language that forever eludes political control.

I called the sky in Crete, House of Sky. Some of the houses,
it was true, were unroofed, thus, filled with sky,

but that is not what I meant. Yesterday it hailed.
We saw stones on the porch. The dogs howled.

The house of sky was coming down to them. An old
woman exited out of her peeling green door.

She wore a scarf and carried a pan of something.
She fussed, the sky reached down into her pan,

sucked up the water there. Spilled it. She backed into the house
again. She pulled the sky into her bundle and tied it tight.

Now she has the wind, which if it is a good wind—not the wind from
Africa
which causes headaches and craziness—will bring good weather.

The waves will roll in forwards, as they should and it will be warm
until
the next full moon, and

if you dream, there will be some truth
to the dream, even if it is truth wrong side out.

Dear Edward Lear,

Since I have been here several windows
such as the one you painted
present themselves as a form of seclusion

a ruin. The people of 10th century Crete
seizing the opportunity to build
monasteries carved chapels in caves

among mountain ravines. After several hours'
hard climbing over rock there is a window
under every shelf where light pauses.

And someone has stuffed his clothes in a nook,
or forged a pocket pillow. All our century
forgets the expense of a saw required

for cutting cypresses as tall as these,
one hundred feet long, the mules pulling
the columns for seven days—expensive

things, columns—along a riverbed,
hauled by a line of thirty yoke
of oxen, each with a bucket at one end,

before history, or Henry VIII, or Galileo,
the mules going down hill,
being stopped with difficulty.

Rina Ferrarelli

My modern connection to Greece is through my sister-in-law, who is married to a Greek. She, her husband, and children live in Athens and

Patras. I also have an ancient living connection, since I grew up in southern Italy in what used to be Magna Graecia. I lived thirty miles from where Pythagoras had his academy. The town's vernacular has Greek words still pronounced the old way, and some of the customs observed until very recently were Greek. The women of my mother's generation wove all the linens for the house, including blankets, quilts, and they stuffed pillows and mattresses with wool. Southern Italians, like the ancient Greeks and Romans, believe in moderation in everything and ascribe to fate the random upheaval against which neither reason nor effort can prevail. They have a sense of the tragic. If this sounds *far-fetched,* let me add that when I went to Patras, people who were not related to me looked at me and said, *"You look like one of us."* Still I *was* a stranger. As an outsider who didn't know the language, who had few associations, and those of a mythical nature, I had a clear focus—the opposite of when I go back to Italy, where sad memories make everything more complicated. In Greece I was able to work with the surfaces, sharp and beautiful in the brilliant light.

Greece: Postcards and Reflections

1

Out of the city, no billboards,
the signs in Greek letters only—I'm way past
when I figure them out.

2

The hills look like they must have
for thousands of years.
The tops, rocky,
a few stands of trees below them.
In the pines and scrub oaks,
the dark green of cypresses.
I think of Italian cemeteries,
but they are planted when a girl is born,
cut and sold for her dowry.

3

Small well-kept gardens,
orchards, vineyards.
Orange and lemon trees.
Pomegranates!
The fruit, leathery and green.
Pistachios hang in festive bunches,
the shells delicately shaded
half-green, half-pink.
I can't take my eyes off them.

4

We stop at a roadside restaurant
open on all sides. Rough-hewn tables
under a makeshift roof.
We order a salad. Tomatoes
and cucumbers, olives and feta cheese.
The daughter who knows English
waits on us. Fresh bread,
freshly-squeezed lemonade.
Shepherds and kings must've eaten like this.

5

From the terrace
we look at the slopes of other hills,
layered and misty, tapering off in the distance,

shimmering silver-green
all the way down to the water
a silver-green inlet of the sea.

A bay of olives!

6

If we stopped long enough,
if we left the road
and cut cross-country
we might hear the sound of pipes
drifting through the woods.

7

What is it that I'm looking for,
what is that I'm seeing, making up?
Could I be content
with a stone cottage, enough olives
and grapes for a pressing,
my own almonds and figs?

8

The houses seem roughly made,
as if each owner had made his own.
Good for a temporary stay. Yet,

shoddy or elegant, even on Pendeli
they have additions hugging the sides,
or basement apartments
for a married son or daughter.

Gift or bribe? a voice in my head
wants to know. Still,
we make no claims, we read the signs
without asking ourselves what they mean.

The Oracle of Apollo at Delphi

I'm surprised to find
more banks than temples.
Thebans and Athenians,
Spartans and Corinthians
and every other city-nation
of warring Greeks
had a treasury right on the spot.
The temple to Apollo was built
above a crack in the earth
where smoke rose
from deep in the ground.
When tyrants and generals
wanted an omen
the Sybil
who was always a woman
was lowered into the fissure.

She was raised to the surface
in a trance, speaking in tongues
which the priests,
who were men, interpreted.
When the Persians attacked
in numbers so great
their "arrows obscured the sun"
the omen was always in their favor.
It was always in their favor
even after the Greeks
who believed the oracle blindly
went off into battle and won.

ALICIA SUSKIN OSTRIKER

The influence of Greece on my writing comes partly through poetry, partly through that other kind of experience that involves landscapes,

J.P. Ostriker

seascapes, food, drink, music, and visible beauty. In college I fell in love with Homer (Lattimore's translations), Aeschylus, Euripides, and Sappho (Barnard's) and studied Greek in graduate school in the vain hope of being able to read the ancients without a dictionary. The very first day I was in Greece I saw a production by a young, vibrant company, of *Lysistrata* in a city park in Athens. The first feminist play on earth! I could understand one word in ten and was supremely happy. Lysistrata is my ideal woman, a successful activist for peace—and sexy too. Aristophanes taught me what comedy is. Euripides taught me never to underestimate the power of passion. *Homer* is better than most novels. Sappho deprives me of breath, and I hope someday there miraculously will be more of her.

I fell into writing *The Volcano Sequence* while looking at a guidebook to Thera (Santorini); the first poem in the book was the voice of that extinct volcano, which was also, at that time, myself, my most destructive self, a destroyer of Atlantis. I have hiked, biked, and sailed in Greece. I drink *retsina* in the spring, wherever I am. *The Poseidon* in the National Archaeological Museum is my favorite sculpture on earth; I would like to achieve, in at least some of my poetry, the clarity, and vigor I identify with Greek poetry, art, architecture, and landscape.

Volcano

Let me speak it to you in a whisper
I am like a volcano
that has blown itself
out of the water

my long stony curve
my melancholiac cliffs
a strip of old hard
exoskeleton

the blue Aegean flows
in and out of me
the tourists come, oh they come
to stand where the lava flew

to imagine how
the earth roared showed teeth
bucked and heaves
to look for an hour

at where the tidal wave began
that destroyed Atlantis
and created a myth
a green good world

you remember

ૐ

A woman looked at my poem. What is a volcano? She wanted to
know. What makes you like a volcano? What would the world be like
without the myth of Atlantis?

the volcano is a crack in the earth
the volcano is a bulge over a crack
a fault line runs under it

something terrible happens
and the magma
coughs out

hot beauty
thick and magnificent rage
so what if afterward

everything is dead

when I was a child
I was an island
a small round bushy island
inside me were many

roots, rocks, ores,
flowings and crevasses wrinkled
pushing like joy, like fear's thin
fluids, like love's neediness

maybe too much
and somehow they all turned
to anger and for years
the lava poured and poured

righteously
destroying all
in its path
righteously

roaring

the myth of Atlantis lets us believe
the world used to be better

people lived in harmony and grace once
fish came asking to be caught

the moon shimmered like a mist
in the hair of women

and because we believe this
we have to blame someone   we have to

step down those slimy stairs

ↄ

finally the lava stopped boiling
it cooled and hardened into what you see
blisters and carbuncles of cinders
rough and dry as the moon

striking terror, mindless
as an army, now it's quiet
except for a fringe of surf
and the sway of water in the crater

ↄ

what is Atlantis
what is the myth of innocence
before and after the kick of time

oh amniotic worm
poor lentil wearing your archaic smile
soft baby rockabye

soon you'll be naked
rock cutting your tender feet
mud and tears coursing down your cheeks

the smell of money like brine
flags and bombs bursting around you
greed like a spirochete eating in

but if there is no Atlantis
no managed dream
how can a person breathe in that nihil air

doomed either way, dear God.

Cretan interlude: Lasithi Plateau

your knees like heavy cobbles
in a town square where men sit outside
a cafe stretching the morning

your hand fills the entire sky
with a blue gauze

you created this caldera now full of windmills
we finish our lunch of olive and feta, we bike the flat dirt roads

mountain crests ringing the irrigated land like a signature
of your name—a bluegray zero

one of your many fists probably a meteor did this
all is verdant fertile now in rows

where earth loosens her dress
more of your signs

༄

the clothing of the island is olive groves
trim vineyards, crags
sudden ruins

༄

the secondary road finds a crest and clings to it
we gaze back over the Libyan Sea

we stop a village on a hillside that drops away
to a wide valley where a woman on a donkey climbs up

a path goats spilling after
like the trains of a wedding gown

find dust-free air
fine emptiness

a plane tree behind the church a spring
a stone trough with six faucets six lion heads

an old man in the noon square at the cliff-edge begs coins
a retarded boy with a tree limb plays horse

an old woman waters her vegetables
a man builds a second story on his house

fine emptiness
fine dust-free air

༄

Knossos

we have dreamed of coming here
and here is this handful of stones like rolled
dice, olive trees like iron

older than Greece, it is our dead childhood
sun clamps down on it
once we were heroes we thought

if we followed the red thread bravely
through damp corridors through dust
cobwebs storerooms armories

to the hot womb of the labyrinth
we would find the brutal horned monster
the bull of the earth

who is your enemy or your twin
throat coughing volcanic smoke
we would steep our hands in its blood

we imagined the goddess
with her furled dress and her snakes
to whom we would kneel

today we learn it is impossible to unearth
what the hard clay surface buries
what time chooses to destroy

GAIL WHITE

The present poem was inspired by a recent cruise in the Greek islands and my observations of my fellow tourists at that time. I was attempting to combine the Greek experience with that of reading the Buddha's "Fire Sermon." In literature, I am a great lover of the *Greek Anthology* and the old plays, especially those of Euripides. I also am much interested in Byzantine Greece and look forward to exploring the country at more leisure.

Boomers on a Cruise

> *"Everything, O monks, is burning."*
> —Buddha

The isles of Greece, the isles of Greece,
where we've obtained on credit cards
one tapestry of silky fleece,
two icons, three amphora shards.

Two noble truths: That life is pain
and that our cravings are the cause.
But here we've all grown young again
and laughter routs the cosmic laws.

On Delos, once a treasure town,
grey lizards flick the drying dust,
where once ambitious Greeks burned down
in anger, ignorance, and lust.

Our ocean-going steel cocoon
spins out the silk of innocence.
Only the water and the moon
bring whispers of impermanence.

On Santorini, once the home
of vampires, we look out to sea
from underneath a bluer dome,
and call this noon eternity.

The sun melts down in tropic gold
like Strega in a cocktail glass.
The moon and moon-drawn tides are old
and, like the dinosaurs, will pass.

We build up shelves against the tide:
our luxuries, our work-out tapes.
But slowly we burn down inside,
and find there are no fire escapes.

RACHEL BLAU DUPLESSIS

The poems included here come from a book called *Tabula Rosa,* a punning title that suggests the "page" is not blank; indeed, that it can be made "pink" by attention to the gender issues in Western culture. Thus I begin with the Greeks. The project of writing culture all over again, articulating a female position through the ages, was a motivation for these two poems. My goal—to claim a voice for women poets in a literary history that seemed to erase or minoritize them—is consistent with the feminist cultural projects that gained prominence in the 1970s and early 1980s. I have chosen actual Greek women poets—Sappho and Praxilla—active at the birth of the lyric voice to try to write the history of poetry in a different way, investigating and transposing some of the terms of lyric. One poem is like a self-elegy

"by" a Sappho (c. 600 B.C.E.) who knows her works will in large measure be lost. The other constructs an imaginary work by the little-known Praxilla of Sicyon (c. 450 B.C.E.), a poet whose two remaining lines are preserved only in the demeaning mockery made of her by a classical grammarian. "Praxilla" in this poem is imagined as answering her critic, Zenobius, again and again, by concentrating on the materials he criticized for being combined in an indecorous way. My work on H.D., a poet deeply affected by Greece and Greek materials, my long commitment to teaching Greek playwrights and thinkers in humanities courses at the university level, and my interest in contemporary feminist work in the classics all led me repeatedly to Greece. Greece is a spiritual and cultural site deep at the heart of our tradition, a site in which one may travel imaginatively, as well as in reality. I have done both; my travels to the museums, temples, and landscapes of Greece have helped form and sustain my imagination.

The Poems of Sappho

Tender pain
flat milk
a chest for holding women's things.
Under the flesh-pink moon
I keep my hand cupped.

Soft bread
fresh milk
so round and uncaring
the clear-voiced moon,
a lyre, guitar, and mandolin.

I lie face down
upon a tender pillow.
Rosy-fingered, moons
two minds' desire:
to be one, to be two.

I want and yearn
but never be enough.
But dry breath and a dripping towel
made me stop;
and over my eyes dropped the dark sleep of night.

Praxilla's Silliness

> *for none but a simpleton would put cucumbers*
> *and the like on a par with the sun and the moon.*
> —Zenobius, Proverbs, Lyra Graeca, III

Almost
rounded moon,
Its unspilling
meniscus—

Light.

Honeyed face of the sibylline
earth.

Everything message, every randomness
twigs fallen just like that   here

bright lined bulging square.

Pepo   pepo   pepo
bird-ripe
fruit of melon, cucumber, squash, pumpi-
kin

slimy-seeded   cries   hot
August bouncing.

Sweet the push push out of the cell

mint watery by waysides
soft-leafed basil
tipped by bushy bracts

cusps of the moon.

Under the fingernails
dirt, flour, yeast

crusts of the sun.

Walk down the road until you go under it.

༄

Dew on the wheat field wells up bread.
Stars, grass, fruit, all variants

Bite down.

The light travels like salt
The dark is thirst
deep shadows
of longing for more light—

But is not the longing for shadows
brightness

earth of the meeting tides?

⨘

Wood white
large white little white
littler fritillaries

wayward

"lords" of air.

Green plums red plums yellow sun
grizzled dotty (newsprint) juice
the drupy fruits

    signz
    places

always russing somewhere
A leaf's moist papery crescent sloughs off.

Of silver-waxy bloom
of cuke uncurls
I sing.

The flea lights brisk upon
one tucked foot in the dark.

Mark.

⨘

Written veins the stones' intrusions
wander
untranslated rocks.

Me goes leaping full and empty.

Now the dead dare coming closer.
All is inscribed,
nothing feeds them,

every day a heavy vulval loaf.

Are you ready
to go down
by the water?

What cannot be said
will get wept.

We live a little patch it doth
go forward
into grief

small lilac leafed
no blossom
white feather, blossom.

᷇

Travel through
picking and washing.
Flesh level, iridescent.

Roads travelled, roads untravelled
often equal.

Heavy as stone, loose as honey
earth
is constantly falling into earth.

So dress for the journey.
Pink for the cave
Pink for the endless stairwell

One hell, two deaths,
three tasteless oatcakes.

～

What starts and calls and whistles
through the long clicking night?

Littoral, on the jot and tittle coastline,
plup,
that the
little tides
catch into gravel, stars.

What I miss most *when dead* is the travelling
and after, stars
the shining sun and moon

crisp cucumbers in season
the apples bright
black-seeded *pears.*

But when I am living, bite hard
into the crossroads

cukies wet and apples sweet
I can sing and I can eat.

～

Bury
unbury

life deciduous as the moon.

Biographies

Alan Ansen

Born in Brooklyn, New York, in 1922, Alan Ansen holds a B.A. and M.A. in Classics from Harvard University, where he specialized in Greek lyric poetry. After attending a series of lectures and seminars on Shakespeare given by W.H. Auden in 1946 and writing a paper that Auden said was the most brilliant he had ever read, Ansen became a lifelong friend of the English expatriate poet, succeeding Rhoda Jaffe as his secretary. Ansen also became a close friend of several members of the Beat Movement, in particular Allen Ginsberg, Gregory Corso, and William S. Burroughs, notably writing the first critical essay on the latter's work, "Anyone Who Can Pick Up a Frying Pan Owns Death." From 1954 to 1961 he lived in Venice, Italy, using it as a base from which to travel in Europe and North Africa. A resident of Athens since 1961, he is the author of several books of poetry, including *Disorderly Houses* (1961) and *Contact Highs: Selected Poems 1957–1987* (1989). Ansen's voluminous notes from lectures by and conversations with W.H. Auden enabled him to compile *The Table Talk of W.H. Auden* (1990) and made possible the preparation of Auden's *Lectures on Shakespeare* (2000).

Christopher Bakken

Christopher Bakken lived in Thessaloniki from 1992 to 1994 while teaching at Aristotle University of Thessaloniki and at Anatolia College. His book, *After Greece*, was awarded the 2001 T.S. Eliot Prize in Poetry by Truman State University Press, and has been reprinted in a Greek-English format by Lagouderas Editions in Athens. His poems, essays, and translations have appeared in such publications as *The Paris Review, Gettysburg Review, Raritan, Modern Poetry in Translation,* and elsewhere.

Donald Brees

Donald Brees was born in the San Joaquin Valley of California. He has a B.A. in Anthropology/Oriental Studies from the University of Arizona where he did graduate study in Entomology. He lives in San Francisco, New York, and Europe, especially Greece.

JEFFREY CARSON

Jeffrey Carson was born in 1944 and raised in New York where he graduated from Stuyvesant High School and New York University. Since 1970 he has lived with his wife, the photographer Elizabeth Carson, on the island of Paros where he teaches at the Aegean Center for the Fine Arts. He also spearfishes; accompanies the local chorus on the piano; and writes poetry, translations, criticism, and travel essays. Four of his books are *Poems 1974–1996* (1997), *The Collected Poems of Odysseus Elytis* (1997), *Forty-Nine Scholia on the Poems of Odysseus Elytis* (1984), and *Paros, Roads, Trails, and Beaches* (1974).

RACHEL BLAU DUPLESSIS

Rachel Blau DuPlessis is the author of seven books of poetry, most recently *Drafts 1–38, Toll* (2001). She has written four books of literary criticism, including *The Pink Guitar: Writing as Feminist Practice* (1990) and *Genders, Races and Religious Cultures in Modern American Poetry* (2001). DuPlessis edited *The Selected Letters of George Oppen* (1990), and has coedited an anthology about H.D. (Hilda Doolittle), an anthology called *The Objectivist Nexus* (1999), and a set of memoirs about the women's movement. DuPlessis teaches at Temple University in Philadelphia and is the recipient of a 2002 Pew Fellowship for Artists and of the Roy Harvey Pearce/Archive for New Poetry Award (2001), given to a notable poets/scholar.

LONNIE HULL DUPONT

Lonnie Hull DuPont lives in rural Michigan where she is a book editor and writer of poetry and nonfiction. She is the author of *The Haiku Box* (2001), as well as five poetry chapbooks from small San Francisco presses.

MOIRA EGAN

Moira Egan has an M.F.A. from Columbia University, where James Merrill chose her manuscript for the David Craig Austin Prize. Her poems have appeared in numerous journals, including *Poetry, Boulevard,* and *American Letters & Commentary,* and have won many awards, including nomination for the Pushcart Prize. For three years she lived in Thessaloniki where she taught and had a view of Mount Olympus from her balcony on clear days. Currently she lives and teaches in Baltimore, Maryland. She is the author of *Cleave* (2004), a full-length book of poems.

LINDA ELKIN

Linda Elkin is a poet and former dancer. Her poetry has appeared in many journals, including *Green Mountains Review, Southern Poetry Review, Willow Springs, Poet Lore,* and the anthology *What Have You Lost?* (1999). She has received an artist's fellowship from the Vermont Studio Center and lives in Oakland, California.

RINA FERRARELLI

Rina Ferrarelli's latest collections are a book of poems, *Home is a Foreign Country* (1996) and a book of translations, *I Saw the Muses* (1997). She was awarded a National Endowment for the Arts grant, and the Italo Calvino Prize from Columbia University Translation Center. Her poems and translations have been published or are forthcoming in a number of journals, such as *Americas Review, Chelsea, The Chariton Review, The Hudson Review, International Quarterly, Italian Americana, The Laurel Review, Modern Poetry in Translation,* and *Tar River Poetry.*

EDWARD FIELD

Edward Field received the Lamont Award from the Academy of American Poets for his first book, *Stand Up, Friend, with Me* (1963), the Shelley Memorial Award from the Poetry Society of America, and the Prix de Rome of the American Academy of Arts & Letters. The documentary *To Be Alive,* for which he wrote the narration and which was shown at both the New York World's Fair and Expo '67 in Montreal, won an Academy Award.

Field has given hundreds of poetry readings at colleges and other venues around the United States, including the Library of Congress; edited two poetry anthologies, *A Geography of Poets* (1979) and *A New Geography of Poets* (1992); and has collected two books of the writings of Alfred Chester for Black Sparrow Press. His essays have appeared in the *New York Review of Books, The Gay and Lesbian Review, The New York Times Book Review, Parnassus, Kenyon Review,* and other magazines.

His latest published works are *A Frieze for a Temple of Love* (1998); translations from the Inuit, *Magic Words* (1998); and a novel, *The Villagers* (1999), written with Neil Derrick. The University of Wisconsin Press is publishing his literary memoirs in 2004. He and his friend, Neil Derrick, live in New York but spend much of their time in Europe.

CHARLES FISHMAN

Charles Fishman is director of the Distinguished Speakers Program at Farmingdale State University, associate editor of *The Drunken Boat,* and poetry editor of *New Works Review.* His books include *Mortal Companions* (1977), *The Firewalkers* (1996), *Blood to Remember: American Poets on the Holocaust* (1991), and *The Death Mazurka* (1989), which was selected by the American Library Association as an Outstanding Book of the Year (1989). His eighth chapbook, *Time Travel Reports,* was published in 2002, and his fifth book-length collection, *Country of Memory,* will be released in 2004.

ALICE FRIMAN

Alice Friman is professor emerita of English and Creative Writing at the University of Indianapolis. Published in twelve countries and anthologized widely, she has produced seven collections of poetry, including *Inverted Fire* (1997) and *Zoo* (1999), and is a recipient of the Ezra Pound Poetry Award from Truman State University and the Sheila Motton Prize from the New England Poetry Club. She has been published in *Poetry, The Georgia Review, The Gettysberg Review, Field,* and *Prairie Schooner,* as well as in other journals, and has been awarded fellowships from the Arts Council of Indianapolis and the Indiana Arts Commission.

JACK GILBERT

Born in Pittsburgh, Pennsylvania, Jack Gilbert has held teaching positions at the University of California, Berkeley; San Francisco State University; Syracuse University; and Kyoto University. In 1986 he served as Chair of the Creative Writing Program at University of Alabama, Tuscaloosa. A recipient of many awards, including a Guggenheim Fellowship, a National Endowment for the Arts award, the Yale Series of Younger Poets Award, and the Lannan Poetry Award, he has published three volumes of poetry: *Views of Jeopardy* (1962), *Monolithos: Poems 1962 and 1982* (1982), and *The Great Fires: Poems 1982–1992* (1994).

PETER GREEN

Peter Green was born in London in 1924 and educated at Charterhouse, in Burma during World War II, and at Cambridge. For ten years (1953-63) he was a London literary journalist. He then emigrated with his family to Greece, living first on Lesbos (until 1966) and then in Athens until 1971. From then until his retirement in 1997 Green was a professor of Classics at the University of Texas at Austin (from 1983 with a named chair) and now holds an adjunct professorship at the University of Iowa (where his wife is also a professor). Both the Southwest and Midwest gave him a feeling for the space and energy of open landscape.

LINDA GREGG

Linda Gregg's most recent books are *Things and Flesh* (1999) and *Too Bright to See; & Alma* (2002). In 2003 she was awarded a Lannan Literary Fellowship and the Sara Teasdale Award. Currently a resident of New York City, she has been teaching at Princeton University.

RACHEL HADAS

Rachel Hadas is the Board of Governors Professor of English at the Newark campus of Rutgers University. She is the author of more than a dozen volumes of poetry, criticism, and translations. Her most recent book of poems is *Indelible* (2001) and prose is *Merrill, Cavafy, Poems, and Dreams* (2001).

CHARLES O. HARTMAN

Charles O. Hartman has published five books of poems, most recently *Glass Enclosure* (1995) and *The Long View* (1999) and three books of critical prose (on prosody, jazz, and computer poetry). He is the poet in residence at Connecticut College and also works sporadically as a jazz guitarist.

ADRIANNE KALFOPOULOU

Adrianne Kalfopoulou is a graduate of the New York University Graduate Creative Writing Program and a Ph.D. recipient from Aristotle University, Thessaloniki. Her poems have appeared in various journals, including *Phoebe, Pavement Saw, Nimrod, Atlanta Review,* and *13th Moon.* Her chapbook, *Fig,* won the 2000 EDDA Poetry Chapbook Competition for Women from *The Sarasota Poetry Theater Press;* she also has published a book of criticism on female discourses in American culture, *The Untidy House* (2000) and has written on various ninteenth- and twentieth-century American texts. She currently teaches Literature and Creative Writing at the University of LaVerne's Athens campus.

ROBERT LAX

Robert Lax was born in Olean, New York, in 1913. While at Columbia University, from which he received a B.A. in 1938, he became a close friend of Thomas Merton, who once observed that Lax "meditated on some incomprehensible woe." Mark Van Doren, one of Lax's teachers at Columbia and also a lifelong friend, carried Merton's observation even further: "The woe, I now believe, was that Lax could not state his bliss: his love of the world and all things, all present in it."

In the 1940s, Lax worked at various jobs, including as a contributing and assistant editor for *The New Yorker,* a film reviewer for *Time,* an instructor at the University of North Carolina and Connecticut College for Women, a freelance writer and photographer, and a screenwriter for Metro-Goldwyn-Mayer Studios in Hollywood. During this period he made trips to France, Italy, and the Virgin Islands. In 1949 he traveled through Europe with the Alfred Court Zoo Circus and through Canada in 1951 with the Christiani Family Circus. He moved to Greece in 1960, living mainly on the islands of Kalymnos and Patmos where he remained for almost forty years. Failing health forced him to return to Olean, New York, where he died on September 26, 2000.

Lax wrote numerous books during his lifetime, published mostly by small presses in Europe, America, and Australia, including *Love Had a Compass: Journals and Poetry* (1996) and *A Thing That Is* (1997). His first collection, *The Circus of the Sun* (1959), was a cycle of poems, fairly traditional in style, metaphorically comparing the circus to creation. With the publication of *New Poems* (1962) Lax started developing the minimalist style that was to characterize his poetry from then on. He once described his slow, meditative approach, which focuses on image and sound and draws the reader's attention down the page rather than across, as "a little like a movie film." Elsewhere he explained that he writes in "rhythmic groups of syllables, which perhaps should be called lines but which as I use them rather resemble chains, vertical groups of syllables (usually common words of striking and universal significance—cut into syllables and arranged in rhythmic and semantic grouping)."

P. H. LIOTTA

P. H. Liotta is the Jerome E. Levy Chair of Economic Geography and National Security at the U.S. Naval War College. He has lived in and traveled extensively throughout the former Soviet Union, Europe, and the Balkan Peninsula, as well as Central and South Asia (including Iran). He has received a Pulitzer Prize nomination, a National Endowment for the Arts literature fellowship, a Fulbright scholarship to Yugoslavia, and the *International Quarterly* Crossing Boundaries Award. The author of fourteen books and more than three hundred articles, he serves on the advisory boards of Estudios de Defensa del Instituto de Ciencia Política de la Pontificia Universidad Católica, Santiago de Chile, and the Research Institute for European and American Studies in Athens, Greece. Recent work includes *Dismembering the State: The Death of Yugoslavia and Why It Matters* (2001); *The Wreckage Reconsidered: Five Oxymorons from Balkan Deconstruction* (1999); *The Ruins of Athens: A Balkan Memoir* (1999); and *The Wolf at the Door: A Poetic Cycle; translated from the Macedonian of Bogomil Gjuzel* (2001). Forthcoming works include *The Fight for Legitimacy: Democracy Versus Terrorism; The Last Best Hope: Legitimacy and the Fate of Macedonia;* and *The Uncertain Certainty: Human Security, Environmental Change, and the Future Euro-Mediterranean.*

LAUREL MANTZARIS

Laurel Mantzaris, only Greek by marriage, came to Greece in her twenties, stayed, and now can't imagine living anywhere else. She is a teacher of English and the mother of four.

DAVID MASON

David Mason's books of poems include *The Country I Remember* (1996) and *The Buried Houses* (1991). He is also the author of a collection of essays, *The Poetry of Life and the Life of Poetry* (2000), and the coeditor of several anthologies and textbooks. His works have appeared in *The New York Times, The Hudson Review, The Sewanee Review, Poetry, Mondo Greco, The American Scholar, The Irish Times,* and many other periodicals. He teaches at the Colorado College and lives in the mountains outside Colorado Springs with his wife, Anne Lennox.

BILL MAYER

Born in Los Angeles, Bill Mayer was educated at Whittaker College and San Francisco State University. He has studied with a number of noted poets, including Jack Gilbert, Stan Rice, and Nanos Valaoritis. His publications include two books of poetry—*Longing* (1993) and *The Uncertainty Principle* (2001)—as well as a number of journal publications. He is also a professional photographer and wine importer.

Thomas McGrath

Thomas McGrath was born to an Irish Catholic farming family in North Dakota in 1916. He grew up with the leftist labor traditions of the 1930s and joined the Communist Party as a young man while pursuing his education at the University of North Dakota, Louisiana State University, and Oxford, where he was a Rhodes Scholar. Blacklisted by the House Un-American Activities Committee in Los Angeles in 1954, he was kept from assuming academic posts until 1960. It was in these years that he began his long poem, *Letter to an Imaginary Friend,* which was published in stages over thirty years (a complete, corrected edition appeared posthumously in 1997). McGrath's other books include *The Movie at the End of the World* (1973), *Passages toward the Dark* (1982), *Echoes Inside the Labyrinth* (1983), *Selected Poems 1938–1988* (1988), and *Death Song* (1991). A teacher, novelist, and film-writer, as well as a poet, winner of numerous awards for his work, McGrath died in Minnesota in 1990.

James Merrill

Son of Charles Merrill, a renowned financier, and Helen Ingram, publisher of a small newspaper, James Ingram Merrill was born in 1926 and grew up in an atmosphere of wealth and privilege in Manhattan and Southampton. While at Amherst College, from which he graduated *summa cum laude* in 1947, he did an honors thesis on metaphor in Marcel Proust, a writer who would prove to have an enduring influence on Merrill's poetry. During his college years he also privately published (through a small press in Athens, Greece) *Black Swan,* his first collection of poems (not counting *Jim's Book,* which his father had printed when Merrill was eight). When he finished university Merrill taught at Bard College for a brief period and then spent the next few years traveling to various countries in Asia and Europe, including Greece. After returning to Greece several times, Merrill, along with his companion, David Jackson, took up residence in Athens in 1955, and for the next two-and-a-half decades lived part of each year in a house on the slopes of Mount Lycabbettos, and part of the year either in the coastal town of Stonington, Connecticut, or in Key West, Florida.

One of the most highly acclaimed poets of his generation, Merrill published more than fifteen poetry collections, of which *Nights and Days* (1966) won the National Book Award in Poetry; *Braving the Elements* (1972) received the Bollingen Prize; *Divine Comedies* (1976), the Pulitzer Prize; *Mirabell* (1978), a second National Book Award; *The Changing Light at Sandover* (1982), the National Book Critics Circle Award; and *The Inner Room* (1988), the first Bobbitt National Prize for Poetry. In addition, he published a volume of memoirs, two works of drama and two novels, the latter of which, *The (Diblos) Notebook* (1965)—the story of a Greek-American returning to his homeland—was nominated for the National Book Award in Fiction. On February 6, 1995, at the age of sixty-eight, Merrill died while traveling in Arizona.

REBECCA NEWTH

Rebecca Newth has published five books of poetry, a memoir, and two books for children. She is the founder of Will Hall, Inc., a nonprofit organization to benefit education and the arts. She maintains close ties with Greece through a friendship with the Middle Eastern scholar, Dimitri Gutas and his wife, Joanna, and with Mihalis Tzekakhs, a librarian in Crete and Athens. She is currently working on an essay and photographs of a garden on Crete from the Venetian Renaissance period, a book for children, and a new collection of poetry with the working title *From the Island of Fyn.*

ALICIA SUSKIN OSTRIKER

Alicia Ostriker has published ten volumes of poetry, including *The Crack in Everything* (1996), which was a finalist for the National Book Award and won the Paterson Poetry Award and the San Francisco State Poetry Center Prize, and *The Little Space: Poems Selected and New, 1968–1998* (1998), which was a finalist for the National Book Award and the Lenore Marshall Prize. Her work has appeared in the *New Yorker, Paris Review, The Yale Review, The Atlantic, The Nation, American Poetry Review,* and other journals. She lives in Princeton, New Jersey, and is professor of English at Rutgers University. Her most recent book of poems is *The Volcano Sequence* (2002).

PHILIP RAMP

Philip Ramp has been living in Greece for more than thirty years, writing poetry and translating Greek literature into English. His poems and translations have appeared in numerous magazines, anthologies, and catalogs over the years. Shoestring Press in England published his collection, *Jonz,* in 1994, and in 1997 a bilingual edition was published by Politica Themata Publications in Athens. His latest collection, *Glass of an Organic Class,* appeared in Athens in 2003. Shoestring Press also has published a number of his translations of Greek poets, including Tasos Denegris, Lydia Stephanou, Manolis Anagnostakis, Yannis Ververis, and Spyros Vrettos. A comprehensive collection of the poetry of Nikos Karouzos is scheduled for the near future and an anthology of modern Greek poets next year.

WILLIAM PITT ROOT

William Pitt Root's most recent collection, *Trace Elements from a Recurring Kingdom: The First Five Books of William Pitt Root* (1994), was a "Notable Book" for *The Nation.* Newer work is in *Atlantic Monthly, Poetry, Rattapallax,* and *Whole Earth Magazine.* He has represented the United States at recent readings and festivals in Italy, Sweden (Malmo, Lund, Gotenberg), and Macedonia (at Struga 2000 he read from a bridge over the River Drim to five thousand people). He has been a U.S./U.K. Exchange Artist and fellow of the Rockefeller Foundation, the Guggenheim Foundations, Stanford University, and the National Endowment for the Arts. His prizewinning work has appeared in more than two hundred fifty literary magazines and one hundred anthologies and has been translated into twenty languages. It also has been heard widely over Radio Free Europe and Radio Liberty. He commutes weekly to Manhattan from his home in North Carolina to teach in the Hunter College M.F.A. program.

BECKY DENNISON SAKELLARIOU

Born and raised in New England, Becky Sakellariou has lived all her adult life in Greece. She has raised a family and worked in publishing, teaching, and counseling; she is also a feminist, an advocate for cross-cultural awareness, and a peace activist. She enjoys her plot of land in Euboia, which is filled with fig, olive, pomegranate, apricot, lemon, eucalyptus, almond, mulberry, orange, cherry, and apple trees amongst the wild oregano, rosemary, thyme, sage, and other wonderful growing things. She also is passionate about skiing, singing, and writing poetry.

NICHOLAS SAMARAS

Nicholas Samaras is from Patmos, Greece, and Woburn, Massachusetts. He lived and studied for years in Thessaloniki, Greece. His first book, *Hands of the Saddlemaker* (1992), won the Yale Series of Younger Poets Award. His new book of poetry is seeking publication. A teacher of poetry at the University of South Florida and former director of the Writers' Voice Program at the Tampa Metropolitan YMCA, he has recently won a fellowship from the Lilly Endowment Foundation, for which he will attend and report on the 2004 Athens Olympics. Another goal is to return to Patmos as annually as possible to work on writing and translation projects.

MARK SARGENT

Born in Olympia, Washington, in 1950, Mark Sargent received a B.A. in Art from Mt. Angel College in Oregon in 1973. In 1975 he founded, with musicmaster, The Impossibilists, a Dada performance/publication group, and later studied Buddhist poetics with Trungpa, Ginsberg, Corso, Burroughs, Philip Whalen, Ed Sanders, Ed Dorn, and others at the Naropa Institute, Boulder, Colorado. In 1990 he, his wife, and son moved to Greece. Publications include *Paint the Goat* (1994); *The Body Prays* (1996), a sonnet sequence; and *Stelae Stories* (2003), a sequence of letter poems. A full-length play, *Call Waiting*, was produced in Olympia, Washington, in 2002. He is also currently a contributing editor for *The Raven Chronicles*.

DON SCHOFIELD

Born in Nevada and raised in California, Don Schofield moved to Greece in 1980 after completing an M.A. in English at California State University, Sacramento, and an M.F.A. in creative writing at the University of Montana. His poems, translations, and essays have appeared in various American periodicals, including *New England Review, Partisan Review,* and *Poets & Writers;* and in journals in Ireland, Japan, England, and Greece. His poetry has received awards from, among others,

Atlanta Review, Southern California Anthology, and State University of New York. He recently completed a creative writing residency at Princeton University as a Seeger Fellow in the Hellenic Studies Program, as well as residencies at the Virginia Center for the Creative Arts and the Ragdale Foundation. *Approximately Paradise,* his first book-length collection of poetry, was published in 2002.

ELENI SIKELIANOS

Eleni Sikelianos' most recent book of poems is *Earliest Worlds* (Coffee House Press, 2001). Earlier books include *The Book of Tendons* (1997) and *To Speak While Dreaming* (1993). Forthcoming are *The California Poem* (2004) and *Footnote to the Lambs* (2003). She has been conferred a number of awards for her poetry, nonfiction, and translations, including the National Poetry Series (for *Footnote to the Lambs*), a residency at Princeton University as a Seeger Fellow, a Fulbright Writer's Fellowship in Greece, a New York Foundation for the Arts Award in Nonfiction Literature, the James D. Phelan Award, two Gertrude Stein Awards for Innovative American Writing, the New York Council for the Arts Translation Award, and a National Endowment for the Arts Creative Writing Fellowship in Poetry. She teaches in the M.F.A. program at Naropa University in Boulder, Colorado.

A. E. STALLINGS

A. E. Stallings grew up in Atlanta, Georgia, and has lived in Athens, Greece, since January 1999. She studied classics at the University of Georgia and Oxford University. Her first collection, *Archaic Smile,* won the 1999 Richard Wilbur Award. Her work has been included in the Best American Poetry series (1994 and 2000) and a Pushcart Prize anthology. She has received prizes from *Poetry* and *Five Points.* She is married to John Psaropoulos, editor of the *The Athens News.*

JOSEPH STROUD

Joseph Stroud was born in 1943 in California. He is the author of three books of poems: *In the Sleep of Rivers* (1974), *Signatures* (1982), and *Below Cold Mountain* (1998). A fourth book, *Country of Light,* is forthcoming in the spring of 2004. His work has been awarded a Pushcart Prize. He lives part of the year in Santa Cruz on the Monterey Bay and part of the year in a cabin in the high country of the Sierra Nevada mountains.

BARRY TAGRIN

Barry Tagrin holds a master's degree in Creative Writing from San Francisco State University. His varied art and teaching career began with the establishment of the Greenwich Painters and Writers Workshop in San Francisco and has included faculty positions with Texas A&M University; University of Texas at Austin; and the University of Navarre in Pamplona, Spain. He has read his poetry and exhibited his paintings worldwide and presented lectures on poetry internationally with the Fulbright Commission. His latest book of poems is titled *The Rain Mistress.* He has been living in Greece continually since 1981 and currently resides on Paros where he is the director of Hellenic International Studies in the Arts, a university study abroad program affiliated with the Massachusetts College of Art.

DIANE THIEL

Diane Thiel is the author of *Echolocations* (2000), which received the Nicholas Roerich Prize from Story Line Press, *Writing Your Rhythm: Using Nature, Culture, Form and Myth* (2001), *The White Horse: A Columbian Journey* (2004), and *Resistance Fantasies* (2004). Her work appears in *Poetry, The Hudson Review,* and *Best American Poetry 1999* and is reprinted in numerous Longman, Bedford, HarperCollins, Beacon, Henry Holt, and McGraw Hill anthologies. She received her B.A. and M.F.A. from Brown University and was a Fulbright Scholar for 2001–02. She is currently an assistant professor at the University of New Mexico.

MICHAEL WATERS

Michael Waters is professor of English at Salisbury University on the Eastern Shore of Maryland and author of *Parthenopi: New and Selected Poems* (2001). He is coeditor of *Contemporary American Poetry* (2001) and *Perfect in Their Art: Poems on Boxing from Homer to Ali* (2003), as well as editor of *A. Poulin Jr.: Selected Poems* (2001). His six previous books of poetry include *Green Ash, Red Maple, Black Gum* (1997), *Bountiful* (1992), *The Burden Lifters* (1989), *Anniversary of the Air* (1985), and *Not Just Any Death* (1979). He has been the recipient of a Fellowship in Creative Writing from the National Endowment for the Arts, several Individual Artist Awards from the Maryland State Arts Council, and three Pushcart Prizes.

GAIL WHITE

Gail White lives and writes in Breaux Bridge, Louisiana. Her most recent book is *The Price of Everything* (2002). Recent work also appears at several sites online, including poemtree.com and hypertexts.com.

PERMISSIONS

ALAN ANSEN: "Cats" and "Moving" reprinted by permission of the author and Dalkey Archive Press, from *Contact Highs: Selected Poems 1957–1987*, Alan Ansen, © 1989, Dalkey Archive Press.

CHRISTOPHER BAKKEN: "Alexandroupoli," "Climbing Olympus," "Dion," "Samothraki," "Terra Incognita," and "Zagora" reprinted by permission of Truman State University Press, from *After Greece*, Christopher Bakken, © 2001, Truman State University Press. "Alexandroupoli" first appeared in *Sewanee Theological Review*, "Dion" in *Western Humanities Review*, and "Terra Incognita" in *Southwest Review*.

DONALD BREES: "The Fox on Paros," "The Hermit of Piso Livadi," "Kafeneion," and "Kalo Pedia" reprinted by permission of the author, © 2003, Donald Brees.

JEFFREY CARSON: "After Passover," "Colossal Wind," "Paros Minor," and "Tomatoes of Paros" reprinted by permission of the author, © 1997, Jeffrey Carson. "Paros Minor" and "Tomatoes of Paros" first appeared in *Poems 1974–1996* (University of Salzburg, 1997).

RACHEL BLAU DUPLESSIS: "The Poems of Sappho" and "Praxilla's Silliness," © 1987 by Rachel Blau DuPlessis, all rights reserved. "The Poems of Sappho" first appeared in *Paper Air* and "Praxilla's Silliness" in *H.D.: Woman and Poet*; also from *Tabula Rosa*, (Potes & Poets Press, 1987).

LONNIE HULL DUPONT: "December on the Ionian Coast" and "Three Marines" reprinted by permission of the author, © 1996, Lonnie Hull DuPont. "December on the Ionian Coast" first appeared in *Rain City Review* (1997) and "Three Marines" in *Meat Whistle Quarterly* (1998).

MOIRA EGAN: "Dear Mr. Merrill" first appeared in *Poetry*, © 2002, The Modern Poetry Association, reprinted by permission of the editor of *Poetry*. "Limnal Hymn" first appeared in *Poems & Plays*; reprinted by permission of the author, © 2002, Moira Egan.

LINDA ELKIN: "Amorgos, "Ancient Game," "The Distance to Katapola," and "Navigation" reprinted by permission of the author, © 2003, Linda Elkin.

RINA FERRARELLI: "Greece: Postcards and Reflections" and "The Oracle of Apollo at Delphi" reprinted by permission of the author, © 2003, Rina Ferrarelli. "The Oracle of Apollo at Delphi" first appeared in *Pig Iron*.

EDWARD FIELD: "Donkeys" and "Goats" reprinted by permission of the author from *Stand Up, Friend, with Me*, by Edward Field, © 1963, Edward Field.

CHARLES FISHMAN: "Andros Night" and "The Light at Ligourio" reprinted by permission of the author, © 1995, Charles Fishman. "Andros Night" first appeared

LIST OF AUTHORS

INDEX OF FIRST LINES